Around *the* World Without a Cent

BY
HENRY SPICKLER

"Railway traveling is not traveling, it is merely being sent to a place like a parcel."—*Ruskin*.

"The world is a great book of which they who never stir from home read only one page."—*Augustine*.

"Travel is fatal to prejudice."—*Mark Twain*.

Price $2.25

Dedicated to Those Who Ride a Bicycle and to the
BOY SCOUTS AND CAMP-FIRE GIRLS
Whose Principles and Ideals are Making Them the Greatest
Human Force the World Has Ever Seen

Windham Press is committed to bringing the lost cultural heritage of ages past into the 21st century through high-quality reproductions of original, classic printed works at affordable prices.

This book has been carefully crafted to utilize the original images of antique books rather than error-prone OCR text. This also preserves the work of the original typesetters of these classics, unknown craftsmen who laid out the text, often by hand, of each and every page you will read. Their subtle art involving judgment and interaction with the text is in many ways superior and more human than the mechanical methods utilized today, and gave each book a unique, hand-crafted feel in its text that connected the reader organically to the art of bindery and book-making.

We think these benefits are worth the occasional imperfection resulting from the age of these books at the time of scanning, and their vintage feel provides a connection to the past that goes beyond the mere words of the text.

As bibliophiles, we are always seeking perfection in our work, so please notify us of any errors in this book by emailing us at corrections@windhampress.com. Our team is motivated to correct errors quickly so future customers are better served. Our mission is to raise the bar of quality for reprinted works by a focus on detail and quality over mass production.

To peruse our catalog of carefully curated classic works, please visit our online store at www.windhampress.com.

AROUND THE WORLD
WITHOUT A CENT

TIME......................THREE YEARS
DISTANCE.....FORTY THOUSAND MILES
COUNTRIES VISITED............TWENTY

AUTHOR WORE OUT
Seven Pairs of Tires. Seven Suits of Clothes. Seven Pairs
of Shoes. One Razor. Two Cyclometers.
Three Lamps. Four Chains.

Earned money by working as acrobat, advertiser, agent, auto-mechanic, athletics, bank collector, barber, bell-hop, bill-poster, buyer, card-letterer, carpenter, cashier, cattleman, companion, cook, correspondent, demonstrator, devil, ditcher, driver, editorial writer, entertainer, eye-doctor, farmer, food-collector, foreman, fruit picker, gardener, grinder, guard, guide, gymnast, hair dresser, hat cleaner, hired-man, hotel-runner, ice-cream maker, interpreter, jam maker, janitor, juggler, laborer, lecturer, lodge organizer, magnetic healer, manager, masseur, messenger-boy, monologist, packer, painter, palmist, peddler, pen artist, photographer, poet, preacher, publisher, railroader, roustabout, sailor, salesman, signature writer, singer, sleight-of-hand, solicitor, stamp-collector, stenographer, stevedore, teacher, trick-cyclist, waiter, window dresser, wood-chopper.

(Entered according to Act of Congress.)

AROUND THE WORLD
WITHOUT A CENT
BY HENRY SPICKLER

IT was somewhere in the Wicklow Mountains on the coast-road between Dublin and Cork. The hour was noon, the day cold and wet. My only lunch was a half loaf of bread strapped to the wheel, which I leaned against a sod fence, and on the easy hospitality of the Island, was admitted into an Irish woman's cottage. I had paid a certain definite respect to the other inmate of the house—a long razor-back sow that came out as I went in. For some pictures which I carried I wished to obtain some bacon, a kindness never failing among the Irish, no matter how poor they might be, little thinking that the sow had also the same pain of hunger and was so soon to satisfy it at my expense.

"From Ameriky!" said she, when I told her of my mission, "whare yez hiv iv'rything to ate and dhrink, and yez come over here to stharve!"

I had been listening and looking. The small chunk of peat lay on the open fire-place, smoking, but as usual not giving forth any heat. A pair of tongs and a wornout hand-bellows lay near by. In the middle of the floor was a puddle of water. An old clock that hadn't run for fifty years and a cheap crucifix were the only other ornaments on a heather-bordered shelf by a dusty chromo of the Virgin.

"Youse look loike yer big and sthrong, why isn't yez home with yer folks, raisin' yer own pig?"

I told her more about my travels—that I was going around the world to see how the people lived.

AROUND THE WORLD

"To see how they live? An' hasn't yez houses in Ameriky?"

I told her we had. Then she "crossed" herself, as a rooster, sporting a solitary tail feather, preceded two old hens down through the window in the cabin.

"Yes," I said, "I am to study people around the globe."

"The globe! Now what's that?"

"Why, you see I mean to go clear around the world. I am going to ride to Rome to see the Pope, and I'm now on my way to see Cork."

"Ter see Cork-k! And yez are goin' ter ride all the way jes' ter see Cork-k! Can't yez see it on the map?"

Some people never see anything or get any place except on the map. She little dreamed of the great value of travel. Her vision of the earth was limited to the few wild hills around her cabin, and the map she once saw in a geography when a little girl. Little did she prize that wonderful camera, the eye, made that we might see the beauties and wonders of creation—that human lens that photographs more in ten seconds than the human mind can grasp in ten years! Though she gave me no food, I was glad I could ride away. Like many others she was content, though her head be as empty as her house, to find out things and get to places ON THE MAP!

Discouraged in spirit and hungry in stomach, I came out to find that the sow had found the bread on my wheel and was swallowing great portions of it! "Can't yez see it on the map!" I was more than half inclined to think that this was the best way to see Cork, or any other place.

I am the man who rode a bicycle around the world without a cent. On leaving school in the year 19—, I passed out of the east door of our home in Polo, Illinois, kissed my mother and sister good-bye, and without a single penny in my pocket, with my face to the East, resolved to keep going until I rode around the Earth and entered our home by its west door.

WITHOUT A CENT

It is a queer sensation to leave home on a forty-thousand mile journey without a single penny in your pocket. My first money was by selling a pair of suspenders for ten cents. My next was earned by pulling beans for a farmer. I was already far from home when my first night out caused me to look for supper and bed at a farm-house.

At the end of the first week I found that by deducting the number of miles ridden I had only 39,726 yet to ride, and I was only a little homesick. I needed some clothes, so I hit upon the idea of stopping at "district schools" and giving the pupils an entertainment. Blushing like a red apple, a pretty girl invited me in at the school where I knocked. When I saw that she was the teacher I told her what I was doing, and offered to tell about my trip for fifty cents. She happened to have that amount with her.

Before riding through Ohio I turned aside to see Michigan. It was in the finest of September, with cream and peaches served at tables, and sparkling water from deep wells. To increase my funds for expenses I had some recipes printed which I traded in for meals and sold.

Automobiles already claimed the street in Detroit, Henry Ford's town. The trolleys ran at terrific speed. Almost daily someone was injured by them. One day a man was run over and cut into a couple of big pieces and some smaller ones. When the motorman came back that way again he found the man's foot, which he held in his hand as a delicate lady was about to leave his car.

"Do you think he'll want it?" she asked, nervously.

"No, he has wings now; but I have a dog at my house."

My first real job was in the Reo Motor Shops, where I worked on sixteen different parts of the car, making some of them myself. As my work required the close attention of the foreman, my wage was low. I could never include fowl in my menu. A Scotch picnic was to be held down the river where a chicken-race was to be put on. I wanted a chicken, so I entered the race. In this race of two hundred yards we were forbidden to touch our bird, to push or pull him. We simply had to keep behind him, hold to the other end of the string, and let him go, no matter what direction he chose. Three of the contestants had shooed their birds to the middle of the race-course when mine had just taken the third start for the same place. As he neared the center field a big woman with fluffy white dress scared him, so that he ran and flew far back to the beginning. The fourth time we started amid the hurrahs and laughs of the crowd. Wibble-wabble, here and there, now ahead, now astern, he crossed the center line and hurried me toward the finish. Most of the others were close behind. Then our racers became mixed up among the strings so that we could hardly separate them. One man got free, and with a big Buff-Cochin was seemingly winning the prize from us. He was all but over the line. But the people helped him too much. They pressed near him, yelling, shouting, gesticulating, when the fowl took wing, circled over his head, and dragged him back to the very start. By this time all of our birds had been unwound, and mine had safely passed the dreadful dress at which he had repeatedly balked. He now shot ahead, while one of the other two roosters joined the first, until both were now apparently out of the race. The two contestants on the right were about neck to neck with mine, when suddenly both stopped. Mine was slowly moving, and in the right direction. In the most flattering tones I coaxed him, making myself big by spreading out my legs and arms so he would just have to move ahead. Ten feet more and he would be over the line. Then the other roosters tried to circle back past their captives. Mine was all but on the line. But his mind was elsewhere. He meant to "bolt." At this moment the first rooster

WITHOUT A CENT

on my right made a jump and a fly for the goal, stopping one short foot from it. Here he imitated the slow "one-step" of my rooster, going straight towards the line. Of course I didn't want him to keep on, and my wishes were the same as our competitors. The holder of the string was so sure he was winning he threw up his hands in a hurrah. But he hadn't won yet. There was still a chance for us. Then my bird with a loud "kuk! kuk!!" turned and carried me back to the half-way mark, when he saw the white dress. In a flash he whirled, shot between my legs and headed straight for the goal. My rival in the meantime had been too eager to win, and in coming within a few inches of the goal he had touched the rooster. For this he was set back to the half-way point. Down the line I came, my rooster on the full run, his mouth wide open for air, his wings whipping the breeze. The great crowd yelled and threw their hats. It was my racer they were watching now. If he kept on my bird would win!

He did keep on. He crossed the line ahead of all the others, and I grabbed him up into my arms. My rivals were out of breath and discouraged. They contended among themselves with their birds for awhile and then, time having been called, the judges gave me my winning rooster and the other four.

TWICE ACROSS GARFIELD'S STATE

I took time to ride twice over the state of Ohio. From Toledo I rode to the extreme south on good roads, with deep patches of woodland, and big barns well-painted. Guide boards told me where to go. The country schools were usually of red brick. The windows were protected by wire screens. In the cupola hung a bell. Charts and globes helped the pupils to understand their world, and library cases were full of books—some of them actually readable.

It was "apple time" in Ohio, and orchards groaned under tremendous yield. Then, too, I stopped at cider presses, filling up on sweet cider; and at creameries, fattening on buttermilk and cream. I had chicken and sausage, apple-sauce, and custard-pie every day.

I could oil my wheel on the run when I rode through the Lima oil-fields. Hundreds of monster circular tanks about five hundred feet apart squatted like setting hens over hundreds of acres. A small amount of sulphur in the oil makes it useless as an illuminant. Paraffin or white chewing-gum was one of the many by-products that were formerly discarded but which now sell at fancy figures. At the mouth of deep wells I tramped in black grease and sticky tar, while lying among this foul stuff were chunks of paraffin as white as snow and good to chew. The crude oil is pumped by steam, one man tending many wells. The oil is forced through pipes for great distances, sometimes hundreds of miles, to the supply tanks. As I rode along I saw hundreds of tall towers over wells that were being drilled one to three thousand feet deep. When done the tower is removed, and if the flow of oil is promising a simple derrick is erected over the well to support the pump and its machinery, all of which is simple and inexpensive.

Near Dayton a tack gave me my first puncture, when my cyclometer registered 718 miles.

To see the Indian Mounds I rode to the lowest portion of the State, where as I sat upon the grassy head of the Serpent Mound the sun was setting.

There was the same old creek. Around me were the awful hills. Here once sounded the tocsin of war, when white scalp dangled at belt of brave. The sun set in wondrous color, gilding the hills with last rays, the hollows in deep shadow. From scores of chimneys rose the smoke of thrifty firesides.

Of all the thousands I met on the road in Ohio but one refused me the road. His neighbor told me he was a wife-beater. After that when I met anyone who refused me half of the road I knew he was a coward.

WITHOUT A CENT

Grapes had all been picked in Ohio, but when I reached Lake Erie, not far from Cleveland, where I lodged at the Salvation Army Barracks, the vines were full, fifty miles of them—Delawares, Concords, black, white, blue and pink grapes. The owners told me to help myself. Though western New York summer is shorter than that of Illinois and autumn comes earlier, the lake water tempers the climate, preventing the fruit from chilling. Into Buffalo I rode eighty-two miles one day and seventy-two the next day, dragging a punctured tire ten miles.

With five cents in my pocket I asked for work on the Buffalo docks. I was to get thirty cents an hour. My first job was in unloading a giant ship of bags and barrels of merchandise. My two-wheeled truck was clumsy and heavy. Soon my hands felt as if they were pulling out at the wrists. When I sought a second for rest the foreman always saw me and yelled, "Get a truck, d—— you!"

I was never happier than when with my cycle. It is the best means for easy, quick, cheap, enjoyable locomotion. The fact that you are the power and engineer makes your tour more interesting than to sit flat, dizzy with laziness, in a vehicle propelled by other energy than your own. It is the glow of health, the color in the cheek, the rushing of red blood through your entire system, the blowing up and enlarging of the lungs with pure, sweet air, the working of the legs and feet, the harmonious balance of every muscle and nerve and brain center, the graceful coursing of the gentle steed beneath you that makes the bicycle the most desirable of all carriages as it glides noiseless up and down the scenic road. Indoor people should take long rides on the bike. Their cramped positions and nervous strains call for outdoor activity. Pale cheeks, dull eyes, thin blood send the business to the rival. A spin on a good wheel is the greatest happiness-getter and success-builder one may find. It is the only doctor one needs.

AROUND THE WORLD

In New York State I had a thrilling ride on what is known as the "Ridge Road," five to fifteen feet above the level, running from Buffalo via Niagara Falls to Rochester. Full of curves, and picturesque, smooth and easy to ride, I wondered how it happened. On my left were the dim-distant waters of Lake Ontario, and I guessed rightly that the lake once reached out here, throwing up this ancient boulevard. "We did not make it; God made it," said an old man in a village near Niagara Falls, where my wheel and I, on the very edge of the swirling abyss, looked down at the foaming waters from every angle.

But the good weather was coming to an end. The whole country had been warned of an approaching blizzard that was due on the morrow. At a prosperous brown-stone house in the country I was received by a grown son. When his mother returned from shopping in a near-by town, her son's welcome was instantly confirmed by her sweet "Good evening!" Her supper was dainty and nutritious. She opened a can of the best peaches that had ripened in her own yard, and that is why I took the third dish, with yellow cream. She evidently had been a college girl or else a great reader and an accurate thinker. Her poise and balance were as pronounced as her house was tidy, and her refinement was contagious. While the wind blew harder and harder on the outside, I nestled my feet in the furzy softness of the big house dog while scanning the magazines under the soft glow of a good lamp. At eight we took breakfast of New York ham and buckwheat cakes, fresh-churned butter and hot maple-syrup. It was late when I set out, but a good path lay ahead of me, and I felt sure I could reach Rochester that day, where I could bunk over night with some school-mates.

By noon the wind had broken into a tempest and flurries of snow suggested more and more violent outbursts. Without knowing it I was being carried along by the gale. Faster and faster came the wind until it was next to impossible to stop my wheel. I turned up my storm collar, pulled down my cap, and took the easiest position on my saddle. The snow never seemed to touch the ground, and gradually became so thick as to hide my view ahead.

The "Ridge Road" winds along like a lazy serpent, always toward the East. The storm seemed to follow it, favoring those who agreed with it. Never did anything so conspire to my benefit as my wheel shot along on its whirlwind flight. My thick, short overcoat, with the suitcase and other packing on the wheel, acted like sails, lifting me and wheel at times from the ground like a feathered arrow. Sometimes on a sharp curve or over some high bridge my wheel shivered in affright at the speed she was making.

I must have been going a mile a minute on a downgrade into a deep gorge. By a sudden lifting of the snow I detected far below a partly ruined bridge hanging over a dashing torrent. I was about to leap from the wheel, but I was going too fast for that and the grade was too steep. I gripped the handles tight as they trembled in my hold. Now I rested my whole weight upon them, then upon the saddle; now I balanced my weight between the front and rear fork as I just missed a jutting rock or leaped a wicked rut. When fifty feet from the bridge I found that the approach had been washed away, leaving a chasm several feet wide. There was one chance in a hundred of my making the bridge and holding my wheel on it until we were over it.

The bridge was several feet higher than the path. As the wheel was about to leap into the chasm I jumped into the air above it, pulling it after me and riding it in mid-air, jerking the front wheel up so as to reach the end of the extending plank, and landing squarely on the other side of the break where the bridge was still intact, bumped but not ditched by the loose plank. My rubber tires held to the slippery

AROUND THE WORLD

planks, creaking and cracking under it as the hurricane dashed me across.

The snow fell faster. In spots the path had filled to a depth through which no cyclist might hope to pedal without the aid of such a storm as blew me on. The wheel itself became clogged with snow, throwing off little shavings that whisked into my face. Town after town passed like mechanical panorama.

Then the lights of Rochester glimmered in the distance. Pushing my wheel down the walks, I asked the only person I met the way to the Seminary. Learning of my trip, he asked me to call in the morning upon his father, a lawyer, who needed a stenographer during the vacation of his regular one.

There comes a time to every pilgrim when it is wise to catch breath and live like others. No matter how good a thing is, there is a dead-line to its enjoyment. Gladstone swung England, but also an ax. The clerk, typesetter and deskman must grease around a car, weed onions or feed chickens. The indoor worker must get out; the outside one come in.

Next morning I went to the law-office of Martin Jones, who at once engaged me as his stenographer. Mr. Jones had been chairman of the Peace Meeting at the Hague, and was the friend of two late presidents. Best of all, he was the father of two boys and of a daughter completing her higher course. I was often at their table, enjoying the table-talk of highbrows as well as the turkey. I was easily persuaded by him to join the Good Templars, of which he had been the Grand Chief of the World. I had worked for prohibition in Illinois at my own expense as a junior in high school, having been beaten by a salonkeeper for making a speech that closed his saloon, so it was easy for me to keep the pledge now that there were no more cider presses to stop at!

During the winter I organized a Shakespeare Club mostly of young ladies, as a notice in one of the dailies remarked:

WITHOUT A CENT

"Young People Organize to Study Works of Bard of Avon.—A Shakespeare Club was organized at No. 12 Broadway last evening to study the drama, under the direction of Henry Spickler, of Polo, Illinois, who is spending some time in Rochester on his tour around the world. Mr. Spickler, who has organized similar clubs in the West, gave readings from the more noted poets. The first play selected for study was the historical 'King John.'"

I had "blown into" Rochester all right!

I boarded myself. How I did like to take my turn at the counter, jollied by eager salesmen when I selected just what I wanted, and went to my rooms with my pockets full of Aunt Jimmy's self-rising pancakes and army and navy beans. When the New York Central & Hudson River milk ran out I used condensed milk of the cheapest brand. "It's just the same as our higher brand," said the clerk, "for our agent told us to send for a supply of the higher-priced labels so that when that kind was exhausted we could paste them on the cheaper cans."

On the return of his stenographer Mr. Jones secured me a position as collector in a loan bank. I made twelve hundred calls. A thousand of these delinquents were drinkers. One hundred were dishonest. Twenty of these dared me to collect the money. Twelve threatened me with personal injury. Ten left the city. Several changed their names. Hardly one got away without a clue that found him out. Some I found in jail. Sent one day to locate a delinquent waiter at a restaurant, I called incognito.

"Your friend," said his fellow waiter, "is in the lockup."

The fraud who tried to evade his honest debt usually faced me trembling. The women could tell a smoother lie than the men, but after a few weeks I could detect the liar and bluff. One dashing fellow who had courted a girl five years to throw her overboard for another, told me I could come just once more. When I returned in a few days he blustered up towards me with, "If you come again, I'll throw you out!" When I called later he forgot, for he met me smiling with a cash payment.

The sons of rich families borrowed heavily from the bank. In a beautiful palace on the boulevard the mother of one of these boys cried as if her heart would break, saying, "My boy is go—ing—wrong. He's in bad company. It's a bad girl. MY BOY IS OFF IN BODY AND MIND, sick PHYSICALLY AND MORALLY!"

"You won't have my husband discharged, will you?" pleaded a frail young woman with three little ones clinging to her faded dress. Of course I would not. A married man could not meet payments on his loan and gave as a reason the purchase of an Easter suit. The real trouble was a second woman.

"Don't talk so loud!" said a man to me in the hallway of a flat; "I don't want my wife to hear."

"How's that?" I asked.

"She thinks I'm getting more salary than I really am," and he gave me a sly wink. He got by better than another who borrowed to get married on. Every time I called he took me outside to explain. When I called next time he tried to usher me into a side room, saying, "Do I owe you for those groceries?"

"Whether or not you owe for groceries," I said, "I'm here to collect what you owe my bank—the money you borrowed to get married on!" He settled.

A similar case hung on longer. At last I went to the wife herself.

"You got your husband," I argued. "He had to borrow money to get you. You ought to help him to pay it back."

"Vy should me pay you vor monies vot mine man he owe vor marry he me?" she asked.

In an old flat I sought one. He had changed his name, skipped out, but had returned again, and had moved his family secretly away. Then I went to his

WITHOUT A CENT

mother-in-law. With seeming pleasure she told me he was living at the other end of the hall.

"Who's there?" piped a feminine voice over the transom, in response to my knock.

"It's me!" I answered; "where's Kimmie?" Thinking I was his chum, she called him out to me.

My sympathy went to these borrowers, dishonest though some of them were, and I was glad to give up my job, resolved to help the workers to earn more money rather than to try to get from them what they have.

"May first I rode out of the "Flower City" past the Eastman kodak home and began clicking off the miles on the cinder path for New York. Slow-moving boats drawn by mules on the Erie Canal, where Jimmie Garfield once was a tow-boy, ran on one side. I soon struck the old Indian trail, and at Schenectady recalled the barbarous massacre when the town was attacked one cold, winter night by savages, who set fire to the sixty-three houses, murdering the people.

Picturesque was the ride down Mohawk Valley, where the river runs swiftly over sylvan falls in a valley so narrow as to afford only little farmlets, while on each side rise precipitous hills with lofty brows. Three times I climbed the summit of these sublime heights, where the glory of New York State shows in full splendor. The surface up there rolled away to a tableland set with pretty farms, while the valley below glimmered in springtime serenity.

THE CHARMING HUDSON RIVER ROAD

On the left bank of the Hudson at Albany I began my ride on our American Axenstrasse, the road leading into dark old forests as sweet as a girl's kerchief, with alluring visions ahead, babbling brooks and glinting glimpses of river and steamer. My cyclometer was clicking off 2,108 miles along this panoramic ribbon, when I began to pass the homes of the wealthy. Of the three ways to see the Hudson—rail, river and

AROUND THE WORLD

road—that of the road is the best. You soon plunge into a series of glorious surprises, past quaint farms and orchards so little and homelike you can almost put your arms around them, while on your right, thick with tangled vine and flower, noble woodlands round the river bank. Soft curling clouds caressed the hills, whose dark green verdure at the summit rose clear and striking above the mists. At Kingston was Levi Morton's rich residence. At Rhinebeck, John Jacob Astor's place. Fifteen hundred feet above the river rose proud "Storm King," rude guard of the Hudson. Rough escarpment of twisted, contorted strata of rock, down which crashed lusty brooks, made my feet press upon the coaster-brake to get a longer look at the rugged beauty. At West Point I crossed on the ferry, an idyllic spot for the young defenders of our country. The enthusiasm of the cadets for my travel project was unbounded. Hardly a scene in all my travels was more majestic. It was here that Arnold, honored by George Washington, bartered to England this most important fortress. The scene is heart-breaking. Washington had come to honor him as his guest. In the house a beautiful wife in convulsions. In the cradle a precious boy. At the door, General Washington! Past the fort he has so lately defended I see Arnold fleeing, a trembling fugitive. Leaping aboard a skiff he rows to the "Vulture" and escapes to London, to die in a wretched garret, insulted, reproached, without a friend.

At Sing Sing I addressed a crowd just outside the high walls of that famous penitentiary, after which I was taken through the shops and kitchens inside. At my request I was locked in the "solitary confinement" cell, where the darkness was as complete as in Mammoth Cave, and where I heard only my own heart beat and the louder drumming in my ears. The ten seconds inside seemed like ten minutes. Sorry for the misguided ones inside, I rode away in the

WITHOUT A CENT

month of May, when the birds and the blossoms were out and the skies were blue, reaching William Rockefeller's estate on my right and John D.'s on my left. Near Tarrytown I found the spot where André was captured, near which was the Irving homestead and Sleepy Hollow. Then I rode to Yonkers, where Washington met Mary Phillips, then into Weehawken, where Alexander Hamilton was killed in the duel with Aaron Burr, every mile bristling with historic drama.

At sunset I rode into New York. Full of slummy children that poured from doors, cracks and windows for six floors up, the hungry expressions of these future citizens looked at me as if I were part of the Hudson River scenery. Three great cities are destined to lead the world—one is London; the other is Chicago; the third is in California.

I rode direct to the Mills Hotel No. 1, where I found a sumptuous structure of fifteen hundred rooms filled every night, with bath, books to read and laundry to use, for less than you are expected to spend in "tips" at a good hotel.

As the coronation of the new King was to be celebrated in London in June, I was most eager to find passage on the first possible ship over the Atlantic. My cash soon dwindled. Answering an ad for singers in one of the big churches, I was hired for the following Sunday at two dollars. Armed with my contract, I returned with glee to tell of my good fortune to my hobo friends, who looked at me as if I were Caruso, promising to divide with them after my first Sunday. After my "coffee and" on Sunday morning, I shined up what was left of my shoes and started for the church. I was so self-conscious that I did not remember what the pastor talked about. But as I had expected to sing at both services, I was surprised when he announced that there would be no evening service that day. On Monday I went around and drew my salary—two dollars—just the same as if I had sung at both services. The people seemed to have been satisfied. Anyway, the choirmaster told me he did not need me any more. I went to the Jersey City Stock-Yards to see if I could work my way over on a cattle-boat. Scores of other young men sought the same job, and the shippers had all the men they could use. But I kept after the head man, who flatly refused an audience with me. When I went into his office in the big shed he went out, but I followed him, and when he stopped to talk to a shipper or employe I was ready to be next. After many skirmishes on my return to the office I caught the shipper at bay, when I poured my plea at him broadcast, telling him I had ridden my bike from Polo, starting penniless.

"Around the world without a cent!" he exclaimed. But remembering that he had signed up for a full set of men he snapped, "We don't need you!" and fled. Once more I approached him, expecting him to show fight.

"We are turning men away every minute," he replied.

Sick at heart, I crossed back on the ferry. That night I met a young fellow who was walking around the world. He was worse off than I, for he had no wheel to carry him, but he had almost ten dollars, the fee each cattleman had to pay for the privilege of crossing, while I had still less. The next morning I took him with me to try once more for passage—this time for both of us. When the shipper saw me he appeared to be still more busy. I waited until he had finished, when I asked the same question of the day previous.

"I can't use you!" he said.

As there seemed to be no other possible way to get across the "pond" at this time, his words puckered my face with painful despair. Yet I did not give up. Soon the boss started for the cattle-pens to select the best prime steers for the fine big "Minnehaha," the finest liner carrying cattle afloat, which was to

WITHOUT A CENT

sail for London on the following morning. I followed him. He had trouble in driving them.

That was my opportunity. Leaping the eight-foot fence, I landed right in the midst of a lot of big Shorthorns as the men prodded them with long spiked poles from the fence. I waved my arms and yelled, grabbed one by the tail and another by the horn, the whole herd moving out of the open gate. I was adjusting my disordered garments when the boss came up smiling, saying:

"You seem to understand cattle, all right." Then coming closer he said: "Around the world without a cent! That's the way to do it." Then in a lower voice: "I am getting ten dollars apiece for such as you working across, but if you'll come around when the boat sails I will ship you free and pay you $2.50 besides, which will get your wheel across."

But I had won his favor so completely I dared to ask for my friend, now coming up, who was also accepted at half the fee—five dollars—when with the two preliminary tickets we returned to our hotel, checked out, had a midnight supper of hot tamales and raw oysters, and roamed the streets among the white lights, glad beyond measure that we were to go aboard the beautiful liner at daylight.

Back at the yards at three, we were none too soon, for the cattle had already been loaded and the vessel was making ready to steam to the New York side for the two-legged passengers. We went aboard and began at once to tie up the six hundred steers to long troughs.

When we came up on deck passengers were hurrying to and fro, looking after their baggage and saying good-byes. The gang-plank was drawn in, whistles and bells sounded, and the great ship began to move. No one in the crowd on shore or on ship knew us, but of all the passengers aboard the "Minnehaha" that morning we were the proudest.

A little work took us down with the cattle once

more, and when we came up we were passing under the Statue of Liberty, with the sky-scrapers dropping into the bay behind us. We were well out in the salt water when the gong sounded our first breakfast on ship. Among the score of cattle-boys were two students from Cornell, a graduate of Princeton, a preacher's son from Kansas and two Jews. Fried ham and potatoes, tea and toast made our breakfast. Then we were divided into several sets to feed and water the cows. Water for them was carried by pipes from the ship's hold, with faucets directly in front of the cows. My duty was to open and close one of the cocks as pails were held there by my set of men and then borne to the animals. We then fed them hay, and at nine gave them a little shelled corn.

Dinner was served at 12:30. By maritime law each of us were to receive three pounds of beef daily, with the bill of fare posted on the ship for us to read. A whole quarter of roast-beef was given us right out of the kitchen oven, and we did our own carving, cutting as big a slice as we thought we could eat. Vegetable soup, boiled spuds, bread and oleo, with tea, completed our first dinner. Several times during the voyage of ten days we had roast turkey and goose, and on the two Sundays aboard our dessert was a half pound of plum-pudding. Yet we were always ravenously hungry. Our beds had been provided down below in what we call the steerage on other ships, but we seldom slept down there. We built rude block-houses with bales of hay, leaving only a low door at one side. Every day these were destroyed by being fed to the cows, necessitating our hoisting up from the hold another supply and the building of new huts at night. Two of the boys were in the habit of selecting their location in the most favorable part of the deck. One night without warning some of the fellows climbed up on their block-house and dropped the topmost bales down upon them. This floating barn, with its six hundred cows, a lot of horses, sheep and

ATLANTIC OCEAN

A Cattleman—"Minnehaha"

Promenade Deck

ENGLAND

Henry Spickler's First English Audience

His Home on the Farm

poultry, was heated by steam at a temperature of seventy degrees, for even in the summer time it is cold at sea in northern latitudes, requiring heavy woolens to be at all comfortable.

Off the Newfoundland banks we had a storm that for three days rocked us as in a crazy cradle, the waves breaking over the top of the ship and flooding the upper decks so that the hatchways and other openings had to be closed tight. Some of the men fell seasick, the cows also, and some of them lay and groaned day and night, arising, however, to eat four meals a day.

Time is announced not by clocks but by "taps" or "bells." A higher officer, usually on the "bridge," steps amidships and taps a bell much like a farmer's dinner-bell, which is at once followed by the sailor "on watch," who taps another and larger bell more vigorously in the "basket" or "nest" on the foremast—at noon eight taps, at 12:30 one tap or bell, at 1 two bells, at 1:30 three bells and so on in sets of eight, with special taps for the "watch" and for announcing the sight of vessels at sea. Eight bells in the afternoon is four o'clock; eight bells in the evening is eight o'clock.

On the tenth day we caught sight of land—the historic cliffs of Dover, that rose higher and higher as we neared the southern coast of England. We passed the little Jersey Island, from which comes that fine class of cows, and from the higher decks we could see France as our ship was towed up the Thames.

IN MERRY ENGLAND

We landed at Tilbury Dock, where Henry VIII built a block-house, and where his daughter Elizabeth summoned the manhood of England to beat off the Spanish Armada. No comparison could be made between the little sailing sloops of those days and our own proud "Minnehaha."

It was so good to touch the ground again. The

English air was like a cold drink of lemonade, and it was the first day of June. The roads were muddy, and as my tires needed attention, my chum and I took the train for the City of London! We entered this train at the side,—a door for every two seats called compartments, where eight or ten could ride comfortably, in private. We were the only ones in our section, so we could lie down on the long, cushioned seats and sleep if we liked.

Your first surprise abroad is the absence of wooden structures, nearly everything being of brick or stone. The chimneys are at the extreme end, and usually end in a tile or two. Every spot in London has been marched over by countless events that made history. Here a battle against a tyrant king, there a bishop burned, or a witch sentenced. You are knee-deep in Macaulay. I sat in Gladstone's chair in Parliament, hung my hat where the lords hung theirs, smelled at the sweet flowers on the bust of Longfellow and Tennyson in Westminster Abbey, became confused as I picked up a little stone in the British Museum on which was inscribed a bill for a suit of clothes made in Egypt two thousand years before Abraham was born, wrinkled my face at a mummy of the Pharaoh, and rode to the Art Gallery, Spurgeon's Tabernacle, and the Tower.

You never get lost in London: you always come back to the place where you started, whether you want to, or not. One morning I made six different attempts to get away from my ABC Breakfast House to ride to Ludgate Circus, a chief business center, for my mail at Thomas Cooke & Sons. But as the streets all ran in curves, crossing and recrossing one another, I came back every time to the place of begining. But London is so charming, you'd be willing to come back sixty times. The streets are Chinese puzzles, but listen to their names: One day I rode through Threadneedle Street, into Petticoat Lane, past the Boar's Head Saloon, to Helen's Place, down

WITHOUT A CENT

Puddin' Lane, to Marlybone, Mincing Lane and Billingsgate.

Refreshing my memory with Crusoe I stood by the grave of Daniel De Foe. In another spot, by the tomb of Mrs. Wesley, on the plain slab of which I read: "Here lies the body of Mrs. Wesley, the mother of seventeen children, of whom the most famous were John and Charles." I went through Eastcheap where Falstaff and Prince Hal rollicked, and rode around to see some of the sixteen hundred churches, where worship was more formal and pious but not so natural and inspiring as that of our own. You must turn to the left in London, and not to the right, as we do in the United States, in passing vehicles. Sometimes I ran into them because of the difficulty I had of changing my habit from right to left. At one time I collided with a cyclist, because of this, breaking the backbone of my wheel.

That which caused me to look the most was the London girl. Three types repelled, amused or attracted me. One was masculine in manner, outdoing the worst in American coarseness. The second was very poor, anemic, ignorant, and with senseless blank stare. The third,—well-dressed, neat, modest and lovable, she drew the attention away from the fussily-robed woman by her plain white dress. Her glance of sweet modesty, wholesome love, quiet reserve, calm thought, purity of soul, good sense, and fair-cheeked health, was an inspiration. The natural gift of the Isle is wonderful hair which on young girls flows loose over the shoulders. It is very light in color, and yet it has the power of playing other colors, particularly that color that suggests red and brown, or brown and red, in such a way that you can hardly hold yourself back from hugging the owner. At certain angles you see a tinge of flame in it suggesting the orange in the rainbow. It is nowhere else in all the world but right there where you see it,— in that waving, moving, changing mass of carefully brushed, fluffy, silken armful of girlish hair that graces the fair complexion of these girls when of the age at which they dream of St. Agnes. Her pink cheeks are surmounted by a color not at all red, but which by some strange mixing of colors, become as indescribable as unsurpassed. The face just between the cheekbone and eye seems to undulate with a witchery of hues that change with the passing moods. In laughter, and at play, this facial beauty is worth the price of a ticket, of which I had many a free one. The eye is mild, soft as a gazelle's and inclined to be very blue—blue as the sea—and just as wonderful in mystery. The forehead is well-proportioned, the chin small, rather retreating, round and delicately poised. The nose is straight, or slightly beaked, the mouth with the full rich curve of the Venus bow. If the Chicago girl is the "I Will!" of American progress, the London girl is the "I Would, but I Can't" of feminine winsomeness. It is harder for her to find a husband than for our American girls, for wars have taken the men. This fact makes her all the more studious of her winning points, and more painstaking in cultivating her personality.

For twelve cents a day I had stopped at Lord Rowton's Hotel for workingmen, where I had every convenience—gas ranges for cooking, hot and cold showers, laundry, dining room and tables, with cooking utensils, and a good, clean bed in a nice room, thrown in. But when my cash dwindled to nine pennies I mounted my wheel. Down toward the Thames, then under the river it went, and out of the great tunnel into a blooming country scene, on a sunny day in June. In America you are "knee-deep" in June. In England you are up-to-the-neck. The country roads were even more crooked than the city streets, and I couldn't always tell whether I was coming, or going. The lanes down which I was riding were taking me into a verdant circlet of summer

WITHOUT A CENT

glory. Every hill revealed quaint and startling beauty, the natural charm of the hedge-rows, the little fresh fields, the orchards and gardens, all teemed with wonders, dense in vegetation and set off by groups of hoary old trees of superb foliage. On and on my wheel carried me until after a slow hour of riding, it ran into the Market Square of a town by the name of Woolwich, ten miles from London Bridge. My chum started at the same time, in the same direction, and got out of a Bus stopping in the Square a few minutes after I dismounted. Workers in the Arsenal, back from their lunch, were standing about, awaiting the opening of the gates to go to work. I borrowed an orange box from one of the stalls, and stood in silence, as hundreds of men, and then thousands, gathered around my wheel over which I had spread the "Stars and Stripes" and the Union Jack. I took a text: "I call upon you young men, because you are strong," and began my first speech abroad. My heart was in my throat, for I had a great audience in size and material. South Africa veterans were there, soldiers and sailors from Egypt, men on furlough from India, plain-clothes men and police, citizens and officers. Intelligent and critical, sympathetic and interested, they challenged my confidence to make good. I spoke very rapidly as the men crowded close and then closer, the stalls emptying of purchasers. Then the whistle blew—twenty minutes after I began to talk—and the men surged toward the Arsenal, dropping their free-will offering. The first coin was a half-penny. It looked like a dollar. It gave me more real joy than the fee paid me since on the lyceum platform. In all I got nearly a dollar in English values.

Then we rented a back room in "Nightingale Vale" that looked out on a vine-clad dell where every morning the birds held a musical festival. Our meals were sometimes brought up from the basement by the good land-lady, and at other times we cooked them on the gas-range. During the week I broke one of my pedals, which could not be replaced, so I had to pedal along with one leg, letting the other dangle over the side.

The paper soles of my American shoes were about all gone, and my pocket was about empty. Rent was due. No food was in sight or smell. My chum became discouraged. In my little bible I read to him: "If you faint in the day of adversity, your strength is small," and "Trust in the Lord, and do good, so shall you dwell in the land, and surely you shall be fed." Then it rained nearly every day. But the less my chum had, the more he spent. He brought home big jars of jam. I urged him to economize until we had more money, but he said he was going to have enough to eat no matter what happened. But he did not seem to realize that we might have the things we needed, if we but went at it right to get them. I was happier here when starving than I possibly could have been back in the United States with plenty, but with no useful future in anticipation. To accomplish my tour was the whole thing with me, and to be hungry sometimes, did not lessen, but only accentuated my desire to accomplish it.

One morning I rode my one-legged bike into London where I found the needed pedal at the American Supply Company, but when I opened my purse from habit I found it empty. "That's all right," they said, "we are glad to help you." Then I went for my mail. A letter invited me to a social, after which I was to be a guest in an English home over night. Another letter invited me to a big banquet of the day before. It came from one of the best known men in Britain, to the most important gathering of the year, where I might have spoken to twenty thousand people, which would have been an unlimited Letter of Credit in the British Isles. But it was past. But I went to the social that night, in the heart of London, and then home with a friend I had met in Rochester. I slept in an old English bed in one of

WITHOUT A CENT

London's old houses, taking breakfast with a real old English family at eight. The Londoners did not open their shops until nine.

I rode back to the Vale for one more night, then rode into the country, still farther, while my chum returned to the City. In a few minutes I was among the farms. In the deep hollow on my right was a brick-yard, and on my left, rising high and dark on the green hills, a dense bit of forest that cut the sky-line at the edge of which stood a little gray-stone church with high stone-steeple, and graveyard behind it. The road swung in graceful curves over bossy hills dipping violently into pretty valleys with green fields and soft meadows on both sides. Hundreds of laborers were at work on one of these farms—men, women and children, most of them picking berries. After walking up a very steep hill that swung in a half circle about a meadow, I came to a second little church with greatly weathered tombstones. A dozen men were making hay in the meadow on my right. I asked if I might get a job there.

"Aye! Aye! Sir, h'I suppose, sir, but the boss e's away," answered one. I rode to the barnyard and waited. The house nestled in a high-walled garden, on the open side of which, was a little pond for ducks.

"Go out with that man into the hay when the whistle blows," was all the foreman said. When the whistle at the brick kiln blew, the men filed down the road and into the meadow where I joined them, turning the grass over to dry, each of us on a row.

"Urry h'up there!" called out the man behind me, but I could not go any faster than the man ahead of me went, which I was doing with almost no effort, for the work was very light. An American is made of different stuff from the average "bloke" in England, so they soon called to me not to work so fast.

"We want this job to last, man, 'ang h'on slow like."

Several times during the afternoon the farmer

drove into the field in his gig on his rounds of inspection, looking sharply at me. He wondered why I would make such a tour, working so hard at common labor, if I had an education and lived in America. At his approach the men worked faster, and at his leaving they slowed down, then leaned on their forks and finally when he passed out of sight to another part of the thousand-acre farm, they threw themselves upon the grass and played cards or smoked. There was no sympathy or personal touch between the farmer and his men, and the longer I worked there the more I felt like doing just what they were doing—"killing time." The weather was so cool many of the men wore woolen caps and woolen undershirts, while one man actually brought his overcoat along to the field and pitched hay one afternoon while wearing it. Yet they said: " 'Ow bloody 'ot h'it h'is!"

When they were thirsty one of the men asked me to bring the jug. It held beer, which I refused to drink.

"Oh, well, we won't persuade you," said a gypsy of the gang. "You'll get a shilling more for not drinking. The foreman doesn't like us to drink." And I did get twenty-five cents more per day.

At five-thirty, when the whistle blew for us to quit work, the men were lying down in a far corner of the field, one fellow asleep. Not hearing the shrill whistle nearby, he slept on.

"Leave off!" shouted one of the fellows, and the rest of us jumped to our feet and started for the house.

That evening I went to the house and asked the farmer boss where I was to get my supper. He seemed perplexed, not knowing what to answer me.

As I had nothing to eat, he let me sit on his doorstep while the girl brought a plate of strawberries and milk, with several thin slices of bread. For the first time in my life I slept in a stable.

WITHOUT A CENT

At three I was awakened to join the merry strawberry pickers before going to work on the farm at the regular hour. Down the dark road I followed a lot of men, women and children into the fragrant fields, the dew like a river, our number joined everywhere by more pickers. When the forty acres of berries were reached, the first dawn had come, and with it the glory of England's rural life that burst into my soul by its overpowering revelation of fresh beauty and tranquillity. In spots a purple graying mist hung over the fields this June morning, such as I had never seen before, with an army of sweet-toned birds—strange birds—everywhere about us, that proved to be skylarks. The berries were the largest, juiciest and best I had ever seen, and as the sale of them in London was limited, the foreman told me I could eat as many as I liked while I picked. A peck measure was given me, and for every peck gathered before breakfast I was to receive an extra pence. The first morning I did not try to keep up to these experienced pickers, but ate berries, and watched the larks as they hovered near the bushes like hummingbirds, singing and twittering with quick, joyful notes, then with wings whirring faster and faster, they began to ascend, straight up,—not in spirals or circles,—but straight us as a ball goes straight, singing with more rapturous melody, until they passed out of sight; descending, after a time, in much the same way as they went up,—straight down.

> When the lark is poising over
>   Big, red berries, bending low,
> And the pickers fill their baskets
>   With the finest fruit that grow,
> Then the largest, sweetest berries
>   Melt and fill my yawning mouth,
> With their juicy, crushing sweetness,
>   Melting in my hungry mouth.

AROUND THE WORLD

From the foul soil comes this berry,
   Perfect, pure and full of charm.
From the grit and sandy earth-loam
   Springs the best thing on the farm.
If I'd turn by transmigration
   Into other form of life,
I would be a big strawberry,
   Just to live the sweetest life.

By the third morning I had caught the knack of doing it. When I took the last row with the two hundred pickers on my left, each on a row, most of them with many years of experience in this work, and many of them expert pickers, some one yelled:

"Look h'at that H'American h'in 'is bicycle suit!"

I drew myself together in one great force. Left-tackle scrimmages on Stagg Field came before me. Why not win this race? I knew that not one of the two hundred had as much energy to let loose, or more trained efficiency. Lightly, but like lightning, I touched, every finger alert, both eyes on the bushes ahead of me. Like whirlwind through the leaves, the berries dropped into my hand and out again into the basket. The few in the far lead sensed my object and picked faster. Others behind them did the same. Still others, falling behind, stopped picking, as they watched the race, knowing they were already out of it. As I moved forward, still others fell behind, until I had moved up ahead of all except a score of women and one man. Then a bunch of these slowly lost ground as I gained foot after foot, passing two girls on rows next to mine, who finding themselves losing beyond recovery, sat down and ate berries out of their baskets, as they watched the race, saying to me, "You can't catch Mary Liz."

These strawberry plants were much bigger, fuller and taller than those I had cultivated in Illinois, the light, sandy soil and humid atmosphere being better

ENGLAND

Berry Pickers

Two Big Horses to Little Cart

ENGLAND

Cricket Game

The Author in English Hayfield

WITHOUT A CENT

adapted to their fuller perfection. Faster, and faster, and yet faster, I went, the berries pouring, in steady stream through my hands, and rounding out the basket. Back at the wagons the foreman received my berries, gave me my tin check, and a new basket. As I ran back to my row, the "leading man" was holding his back with both hands. Five women were ahead of him and me, picking like mad. I geared myself to the third speed. One by one I passed ahead of the women just behind the man, and I evened up to him, to leave him in the lurch when he went back to check in his berries.

One hundred and ninety-five pickers were behind me. That was something. Five only were ahead, but these five had to be overtaken, and then passed. Soon one of these fell behind. Only four were ahead of me now. In a few minutes I had passed one of these. Only three were ahead. Full day had now begun to dawn as the sun raised out of Kentish hills on our left. If I could but gear myself to a fourth speed, the race would be brief. I ate no berries. I heard no skylarks. Two more dropped back. Only one remained,—Mary Liz, known for her speed in all that country, and never known to have been beaten in a berry race. Her row was close to mine. I could hear her breathe. From now on I took no time to breathe. The race lay now between two of us, an English woman, and an American man. Then my teeth went tight like a vise, as I went to the "Nth" speed. My mind was in every part of my body. I no longer looked for berries, but just imagined them there, and took them, pinching them off just right at the first grab, reaching for others, and still others, as I had mapped them out ahead, avoiding the least unnecessary movement, and economizing every atom of energy. Every one of the one hundred and ninety-nine watched the race, most of them standing,—every one except two or three who vainly sought to regain what they had lost,—from ten to thirty feet. Chance misses in the hills might bring them up again, but the Englishman, in planting berries as in doing anything else, did it right. Every row was much the same.

My third basket was filling. I couldn't move ahead fast enough. I hadn't taken a full breath for ten minutes. Soon we were neck to neck. With less movement and more berries, I put every ounce of strength and skill into my picking. Confident, too, that I was going to win, my added speed set me ahead of her, which made her only the more determined not to let me win as she tore the plants, and moved up with amazing speed. She even threatened to pass me, and unless she had caught her second wind, as I had done, I was still safe. The race would be over in a few seconds more. Many of the pickers had come up to that part of the field where we were picking so as to witness the "finals." The last twenty feet I made without taking a breath. When I straightened up for a full breath, Mary Liz was yards behind me, and her basket was far from filled, while mine was running over.

For a whole week I drank no water, but ate strawberries instead—about two gallons every day. During the week I spent but six cents for food, mostly bread,—a two-pound loaf for four cents, or two English pennies. Volunteer potatoes, onions and other vegetables, were found on the farm, which with the skimmed milk brought me by the maid, furnished me a good table at no expense. At the end of the first week I was paid a pound in gold, and some silver pieces of one, two, and four shillings each.

I cooked my meals on a rude fireplace of bricks and sheetiron and although I built this stove right near a strawstack and a building covered with thatch, because of the almost constant dampness there was no danger of either catching fire. At this time I wrote my chum in London, telling him of my good luck, when he came out, his shoes worn to shreds. He had

WITHOUT A CENT

pawned his valise, extra clothes and watch, and had spent the last penny. That night we cooked supper around a roaring fire, in a drizzly rain. "I wish I were back in Kansas in the old rocking-chair," he said. The next morning he went with me to the berry patch to "fill up," and to earn his first English money on a farm.

I had changed my headquarters from the stable to the granary, just above the chicken house, reaching it by an outer stair. The first bin on my right I made into a dining-room and pantry. My cellar was above my head, where suspended from the ceiling, I kept the bread and other food. The next bin was my bed-room. A third held my bike, and a fourth was my spare-room. My friend now took this room as his own, and soon saved up enough money to reclaim his pawned goods.

We often went to market. In the butchers' stalls little cards were tacked to hunks of bacon, as "Nice and Mild," "Prime Breakfast," "Try Me." To read them made us hungry for the juicy, English bacon. From the late strawberries and raspberries I made jam, some of which I sold to workers on the farm. In the meadow I gathered three kinds of mushrooms which did more to supply my table during August and September, than anything else. Frogs also were abundant.

After the berries came the cherries. The boss selected me to guard the trees from vandals, for as they were of the large, sweet variety, workers in the fields and strangers passing on the road looked upon them with covetous eyes. The choicest of these I picked for him, eating what I liked, and preserving such of the poorer ones as he discarded, for myself. But my chum soon wearied of the work and returned to London, and with the aid of the U. S. Consul, caught a boat for New York. As he was without a college education or a substitute in mental training, he found little to interest him.

One rainy night a little boy of one of the foremen dropped in and dined with me. The rain fell steadily, and bedtime found him still with me. Not suspecting any trouble, I let him stay. But his father had come home intoxicated, and began to beat up his household, this boy coming to me. I had fallen asleep when I was awakened by unearthly yells and curses:

"H'open that bloomin' door, you H'American!" roared the drunken bully of a father. Half awake, I staggered to the door, upsetting a big pail of water over my feet.

"H'if you don't d——n soon h'op—h'op—h'en—that door, h'I'll show you! H'is my lad up there?"

"Yes, there's a boy up here."

He was coming up the stair, an old rotten one, and he didn't know that two of the steps near the top were weak and rotten. When he reached this place he dropped through it to the pile of tile and rubbish below, jabbering oaths as black as the night. The kid was now crying as if his heart would break.

"That's my dad," he choked; "'e'll kill both h'of us."

I was sharing the same opinion, as the third time the mad father climbed the broken stair, and three times fell through it, each tumble increasing his fury. Knowing that my trying to keep his boy from him would only add to his insane rage, I helped him to get out and down over the rickety steps, to his father, who at once fell to beating him.

During most of the time I earned a dollar, or four shillings, a day. For pitching oats with a big Irishman I was paid $2.50 a day. For cleaning ditches I was given the entire job at four cents a rod, cleaning easily a hundred rods a day.

One afternoon as I chopped into a heavy bunch of grass my knife struck something like a solid cushion. I had mowed right into a nest of hedgehogs or porcupines, the first I ever found in their natural haunts. I could hear the wee cries of the little ones,

WITHOUT A CENT

which at first I supposed to be made by kittens or hares. In the nest were little yellowish balls, and over them, for protection, was mother hedgehog, rolled up in a ball, herself, with the sharp spines or needles sticking out savagely in every direction, some of them pricking the little babies and making them cry, for while they, too, had rolled up, their skins were so much thinner, and their needles so much shorter, they had poor protection from the long, sharp spines of the mother; and each of them, having rolled up like a round ball in the nest when I struck it with my cutting-knife, were torturing each other with these same spines. The mother's armament was sufficient to withstand the attack of any dog, and its safety was in lying still, rolled up like a ball. When I tickled its back with a stick, it slightly unrolled, peeped out with its little head from among the sharp, gray quills, showed for an instant four little legs too small to run fast, or to fight an enemy, then rolled up again, and was to all appearances as dead as a rock.

Another discovery was the English bumble-bee. At first they gave me great fright by their buzzing warning, and I would climb out of the ditch and run, expecting them to pour after me. The noise they made as they rolled out like yellow-jackets, was terrifying, but on returning to the spot I found that these bees never left the nest, but just rolled around on top of the ground fanning the air. At last I ventured right up to them. Then I got down right over them, expecting surely to be attacked by them. I stirred up the nest. I rolled them over. The bees were only bluffing. At other times some of them circled about me a moment, then went whirring over the fields.

Although their honey was mine to leave or take, I always left it and the nest unmolested, for one of the crimes in America is to allow unthinking boys and men to kill off our American bumble-bee, without which there could be no red clover, for only the long tongue of the bumble-bee can reach down to the bottom of the honey-well in the red clover, the doing of which fertilizes the blossom.

Another insect I found that was harmless looking but frightfully dangerous,—the earwig,—looking much like a cricket, having a long, reddish body, with short legs, that prevent it from jumping like our American cricket. This insect crawls into the human ear and from there works its way into the inner ear, and from there up into the brain. Farm-hands, and others, frequently suffer a terrible death from them. We always took care when lying down in the straw, or upon the ground, to see that no earwigs were there, and when we found them we killed them on the spot. Once in the ear, it holds on like a leech, and can be removed only with difficulty by a skillful doctor. If left there it continues boring into the inner ear, thence to the head, when the victim goes mad, unable to endure the awful torture, and dying in the utmost agony, when the earwig reaches the brain. To be safe from them we were careful to wear cotton-batting in our ear-lobes, to buy which I inquired of a young girl at the notion store. To my surprise, she handed me a spool of thread. I explained that it was not thread that I wanted, but cotton, to put into my ears to keep out the earwig. Her mother then came to the rescue. Cotton, over Britain, means thread.

Many common things had new names to me. The accent of vowels and syllables, particularly by the unlettered, is also different, and unless the clerk be well educated, you can scarcely converse with him or her. Day is pronounced dai; gray, grai; "H'I was Mai-Queen," said a pretty girl at the Sunday School, when I asked her if that custom was still kept up in England. Her "May" sounded to me like "my."

But the names of things were still worse. A horse-blanket was a rug; a wagon on a farm was a van; a cultivator was a brake; a railway coach was a car-

WITHOUT A CENT

riage; a freight train was a goods-train; a man told me he was a driver. "Horses?" I asked. "No!" he answered, offended, "locomotive!" Conductors were guards. Locomotives had no big head-light, but only one or two small lights on each side of the front of the boiler. There were no "cow-catchers" on these locomotives. A teacher was a school-keeper; a dairyman was a cow-keeper; a bakery was a bake-house; a hardware store was an ironmongers; a dry goods store was a drapers; a notion store was a haberdashery; a balky horse gibes, and whether you want either oats or corn fed him, it is always corn. The boy who plays truant "skips the dollie." "Washing and Mangling" means Washing and Ironing; condensed milk comes in tins, not cans; it is five pence the person, not five cents each. Butter may be bought at the store, salted or unsalted, and at the same price. Sunday School pupils were flogged just as were pupils of the public school.

I went to the dentist to have a tooth filled. The sign over his door read: "Stopping and Scaling," which meant Filling and Cleaning. I had a tooth stopped, and all of them scaled, but for the last time by an English dentist. I went to the barber to have my hair cut. A man and a boy were running three chairs,—ordinary, straight-backed chairs. He cut the long locks from the right side, then went back to the man he was shaving, ignoring me. After he took the whiskers off the left side of the victim's face he came back to me, while the boy lathered the other side of the man's face. Then he took off the right whisker, and returned to me. The third time he came back to me I was asleep.

On the day the king was to be crowned I rode into London at five in the morning and secured a position in Trafalgar Square where I was very near the King and Queen when they passed in their Royal Coach, at three in the afternoon, not one of the tremendous crowd daring to give up his space during all that time. At the King's Dinner given shortly after, I sat on the same platform with the Lord Mayor of London and his beautiful wife, shaking hands with them and chatting with them. "You are to see England from your wheel?" asked his wife in her sweetest manner. When they left they both shook hands with me, again, and I can feel the pressure of the little gloved hand to this day. Her winsome sympathy did much to help me on my tour from that day on. For the Lord Mayor of London is an important functionary greater in authority than the King himself. Costumed in his official robes of faded orange bordered with heavy fur, and encircled by a heavy chain of gold over the shoulders and back, a mace carried before him by a courtier and other attendants of the Court, and with him the great Bishop of London with richly gowned wife near him was a picture of modern human power united with all the royal romance of mediaeval history.

On the last day of September I rode for Canterbury over the path of the Chaucer pilgrims, the road and lanes like meandering boulevards, where a twenty-mile spin before breakfast was a luxury. Great spreading oaks and lindens grew in the pretty fields. Up-hill and down, winding around dreamy hawthorne hedge, over old stone bridges, through deep, fragrant woods, skirting meadows where yeomen pitched hay on queer old wagons, and the kiddies played, with history hovering like the London fog, over every bit of ground I rode over, where some hero died for human rights, a king was defeated, an army was routed.

Six miles out, I wheeled up to the "Three Squirrels Inn," on Saturday night, where in the olden days the Pilgrims stopped,—as I did. With no parlor or office, the bar-room is the meeting place of guests. Unlike anything in America, there is a cordial hospitality in these old inns. You are made a deal of, and you become quickly acquainted with everybody. But to stop at THIS inn, haunted by the shades of gray

WITHOUT A CENT

old Chaucer Tales,—to snuff your candle in a room occupied by these old worthies!

A woman illumines the forecasting shadows of every ambitious man. The orator rises to the sublime peaks of majestic utterance on the wings of fancy for some sweetheart. The musician swings wide the gate of song by the key of love. So I saw Canterbury, inspired by an old lady teacher in Shurtleff College.

Thousands of worshippers had already gathered in the great Nave, at the upper end of which I was seated, on an elevated portion on a scarlet carpet, with others, who seemed to have been favored. My bicycle suit attracted too many eyes for my own comfort, until the unexpected happened. A man, with his wife, sat next to me, at the very edge of the flight of wide-step stairs. Suddenly, with a movement and noise that was startling, the leg of his chair slipped off the edge of the step, when both man and chair toppled over into the lap of an elderly lady with goggled eyes. From here he dropped on his knees in front of her, in a beseeching attitude too ridiculous to prevent laughter in that sacred place. Flinging his arms wildly to regain his balance, he took a football dive into Goggles' ample lap. His ludicrous sprawl was an easy mark for two-thirds of the great congregation, and a target for the assistant ministers, several deans and priors, two canons, and the great Metropolitan Archbishop himself on a salary of five hundred thousand dollars a year, all of whom indulged a look of humor. To make it worse, everything was at a standstill when the gentleman fell. Helped back into his chair by his wife and me, she soothed him by whispering into his ear so that many could hear her that he ought to know better than to sit so near the step. Relieved thus of much of his embarrassment, the service in the High Church of England was resumed by the speaker upon the theme: "The Need for More Definite Anticipation of

Heaven." He said that the present must be fully developed if the future was to be fully realized; that Heaven was a going on, a realization of an ideal, a resurrection of long-buried hopes. After the collection bags passed the Archbishop raised his hands and pronounced upon us a one-hundred-thousand-pound benediction.

That evening I addressed two open-air audiences of five hundred and a thousand each, taking up "collections" myself, and being interrupted by a cop who asked me if I were a Mormon from Salt Lake.

Most of the Nave was built in the fourteenth century when Richard the Second sought to rule against his cousin, Henry the Fourth. To a height of three feet the walls are of the tenth century, with Norman designs in them. The pillars rest on square bases, crowned by square caps, with narrow, semi-circular windows. I saw the old coat of the Black Prince, and the spot where Thomas a Becket was murdered. In the upper nave I translated at sight, as any beginner in Latin might do,—"In eadem laetae Resurrectionis spe His requiescunt Catharina, filia Nicolai Sympson,"—took a last look at the wonderful thirteenth century glass windows, and rode to a monument to forty-one martyrs burned there for their faith, among the names being Henry Lawrence and Annie Albright. Over the old Roman road eight to twenty-five feet wide, I pumped up Gad's Hill where Falstaff played the brave; went through Dickens' old home, sat in his armchair, and laid my hand on his desk where he wrote of "Nell."

At midnight I was still riding on a good road north of London where the people I passed greeted me with friendly tone of voice. Refilling my lamp I rode till two, when it again went out, compelling me to walk rather than to break the law. Sleep began to overpower me. The towns were all shut up. Then rain began to fall. There is a vast difference in the states of mind before and after midnight, on a strange road. Weariness is then a torture. The moaning wind cries in your ears with hideous shriek.

At a big gate through a hedge-row I found an overarching covert made at the junction of the road hedge and another, forming, with the addition of a thicket of hawthornes, a perfectly dry den, protected from the cold wind and dripping rain. For a second a match showed me the "lay" of the situation. A better bed could hardly be found out of doors. But evidences of other road men were there ahead of me, such as fresh newspapers and trampled grass, so I had no inclination to venture back. A tourist had been beaten and robbed of his wheel and money shortly before. Even now one or more of England's eighty thousand tramps might be resting in there, and might take my wheel as I slept. So I came out on the road again, sleepy as I was, preferring to be safe than sorry.

The tea-pot is always a-boil in the Lodging-House, and the toasting fork hangs by the iron grate. Each guest buys his own food, and cooks it. This is the resort for the farmhand whose employment has been for the summer, the country tramp, or the native tourist, the strolling musician or acrobat, and the roving gypsy. Eating, drinking, talking, reading and sleeping,—besides seeing the local world,—is the profession of most of these guests. They know every nook and corner of the British Isles and they discuss gravest questions of finance, politics, or authorship.

Like an undulating ribbon of green-bordered silver, shaded by magnificent old trees that almost touch at the top, the road carries you in and out of disappointing Cambridge, along the lazy creek they call a river, with little ferries bumping their nose into the other bank before it has cleared from the side you get on, boat-houses occupying every available dock space. For centuries master minds from many continents had enrolled inside those walls, in student and teacher, whose influence had returned in later generations to bathe once more those gray-worn walls with time-honored devotion, and settle again upon outgoing graduates,—the distilled essence of England's literary glory.

Guide-posts and a road map made easy riding to Bedford. I was in Bunyan's town before I knew it. The next day, Sunday, I walked to Elstow, a mile or so to the side. In my sightseeing I have the tourist's enthusiasm for historic spots, and my most exhilarating moment is when I am about to see the long expected sight. At the post office I was invited to take tea by the post-mistress—in John Bunyan's post-office! She and some ladies were already at the table, so I sat with them and sipped black tea with lump sugar and yellow cream, and some very thin slices of bread spread thinly with butter. O Bunyan!

I saw the original document for his arrest, the old jail doors and his chair. That night I preached in the old Moat Hall where years before, the Bunyanites had fled fiery mobs. This audience was the easiest to talk to of all my world assemblies, and at the close I stood by the pulpit while every one filed past me, shaking hands with me, a small coin in every hand, until my pocket was full of money!

I liked Oxford, but students here had either big bank accounts or scholarships. One of these milk-fed pets had so many scholarships he couldn't spend all the money, and had on hand at the end of the year, fifty pounds. The haze hanging over the buildings, the heavy fogs, the frequent rains, the old buildings themselves, seem to curb the modern idea of "push." The cue seems to be to take things easy. The very pens used by the students were turkey quills. So I had been with "Tom Brown at Oxford."

In a Riot

On the way to Birmingham, I had the surprise of seeing the grand palace of Blenheim, as it suddenly burst upon me in a most enchanting forest of oaks, lindens and maples. The place seemed so big, so

ENGLAND

Four Tons of Spickler's Cabbage

Home of the English "Blokes"

IRELAND

Passing Island—Atlantic

WITHOUT A CENT

lonely, so exclusive, I would not want to live there. No dogs, no kiddies, no cows, were to be seen. I did not envy the Miss Vanderbilt who left our land to live here. Near this estate I came upon the old home of George Washington, riding through the delirious forest of Arden, into Stratford, where, in Shakespeare's home, I wrote my name, right below Walter Scott's!

Sunday night in Birmingham I was invited by a City Councillor to speak from his wagon in the "Bull Ring," a big open square in the center of business. It was nine when we mounted the wagon-pulpit amid a sea of upturned faces running into the ten thousand. He first harangued the crowd, which grew turbulent under his way of saying things. "You'r a liar!" "Pull him down!" hurtled from the maddening crowd. He was breeding a riot, and I was helpless in the midst of it. I expected the wagon to be overturned, for the mass of people surged against it, squeezing it until it creaked. Men began to climb into it, and two rowdies were in the act of taking hold of the councillor when the riot-call squad of police arrived, and led the bullies away under arrest. If only the councillor would stop, I thought, and give me a chance to talk to them. I wanted to pull his coat-tail to make him sit down. But he represented the great City of Birmingham, and I was only an invited guest. Finally he began to stop in his Irish way, for he was Irish. I had remained cool and collected, my eyes on the crowd, and the speaker. The more they had raved the more I had calmed.

I was introduced as an American tourist. At once I was on my feet, and instantly I felt the irresistible sway of hitherto uncontrollable passion subside into curiously interested gaze. Before I had said a word I was master of the ten thousand:—

"You have all heard of Abraham Lincoln, that good friend of the common people. I come from his home in the great Mississippi Valley, in Illinois, that great

State of the United States of America!" I was ready for anything, from a shower of bricks to applause. I knew that a sermon would be the last thing that multitude would stand for, so under striking anecdotes of American life, I hid my points of discussion. A gentle calm suffused my hearers. Not a soul moved in his tracks. There was no sound beyond that of my own voice. It was a deathlike silence. The faces blended into one great sheet of paling whiteness, as with mouths open, and heads forward, they listened to my words. The ten thousand stretched back so far on all sides of the wagon I was forced to speak with such vehemence as to quite deprive me of the use of my voice for one week. An offering was taken at the close, which was to be mine, but the Councillor changed his mind after he got it, and kept it.

On another occasion as I was being introduced, the Chairman said: "I have heard many speakers in the Bull Ring, but I have never seen a crowd as still as when this American traveler spoke there on Sunday night. Twice I found myself staring, with mouth wide-open. I didn't know where I was." So, if I didn't get any of my collection, which was a big one, my vanity was touched on hearing these words.

On the morning of November 11 I went to the Post Office and sent a message over Mr. Cadbury's private wire, at his expense, asking an interview. Almost instantly the answer came that I could not see him. I regretted it, but as he paid for my message, I wired him again, asking if he could not see me on the following morning. He could.

To my surprise, the office buildings and factories were low, of rustic beauty, adorned with summer foliage, in the midst of parks and gardens. In a soft chair I was seated by a blazing hearth with the renowned George Cadbury on my left side. His first look I shall never forget. It went right through me. But in that single look that great man had taken my measure. Balancing, piercing, keen and businesslike, sympathetic in his bearing, frank and dignified, I would pity the trifler who would seek a moment of his time. His greatest impression upon me was his utter abandon, and though kingly in reserve, his whole soul seemed to fuse into mine,—this man who had at first refused me audience! When I told him how I came to start on my tour without a cent in order to better study the world and its needs, he raised his eyes in prayer, and then broke the stillness with: "I will give you a five pound note."

Maybe he heard about my speech in the "Bull Ring" and of the misappropriation of funds by the Councillor. Well, it sounded like five hundred thousand dollars to me. He went to another part of the building, and in a few minutes returned with five pounds in gold, equalling twenty-five dollars American.

"I have always had a hobby," said he, as we sat there looking into the fire, "that grew into this village. My personal and official work among people have taught me that in England, at least, something had to be done toward bettering their conditions if the country was to remain in its rank among nations. I think it is the duty and privilege of the capitalist manufacturer to take care of his workers, to treat them well over Sunday, as well as on week days; to see that those who have helped him to riches should themselves have comforts and true happiness; that employers usually were selfish, caring only for the profits derived from labor irrespective of conditions, physical, social or moral, of their servants." So I had met this meek Quaker, maker of chocolate and of character, owner and editor of the brightest London Daily run on the Golden Rule, Sunday School Teacher, Statesman, Labor Leader, Preacher.

I went through his model village of five hundred houses with an annual income of twenty-five thousand dollars all turned back into the village for further development. It was a walk through fairyland, a song in architectural harmony, where no two houses were alike, with beauty and comfort in the highest degree. The tenant had eight hours for work, eight hours for recreation, and eight for sleep. On the first floor of the smaller house was the living room or kitchen, with bath in the floor, sixteen feet six inches by eleven feet, then a wash-room seven feet square, a pantry with a bay-window opening on a scenic view, and a reception room thirteen and a half feet by eleven. A lobby leads to different parts of the house. On the second floor were three bed-rooms and a linen closet. That the rich may not congregate by themselves, the smaller houses were scattered among the larger. Apple, pear and plum trees grew on the lawn, with linden, holly and other trees in the street.

Mothers brought their children to a fairy playground in the care of matrons while they returned to their work. Swimming and boating pools, with athletic fields, and a gym for boys and girls, with free training by experts, were in daily use. One-tenth of all the ground went to parks and pleasure resorts. When I saw this fragment of Heaven fallen to earth I believed more than ever that the Kingdom of God is with men,—and within us; that we should set such principles to work, now, as will tend to bring comfort and happiness to us all, by our own individual efforts.

On the eve of leaving Birmingham I was a guest at the yearly Banquet of the survivors of the Balaklava War immortalized by Tennyson's "Charge of the Light Brigade." I had never expected to see one of these heroes, much less to have the great honor to dine with them, and to hear two of them recite the "Charge." Though eighty years old, these boys were rosy-cheeked, robust and handsome. Six hundred went into that horror, and after a few minutes came out again, all that was left of them,—one hundred and ninety-eight.

WITHOUT A CENT

The greatest power for temperance in Great Britain I found to be the Good Templar Lodge. Almost nightly I visited one of these Lodges, where refreshments and social games were enjoyed. The women brought their knitting, and when one of them arose to second a motion, her long needles kept flying through the Suropshire or Lancastrian wool. I found no "Little Red School House" in England, and there were no real American High Schools. An element of weakness was the two-system schools of the Nonconformist Church, and the "Church." None of these schools welcome visitors, and my getting into them was due to my nerve rather than to an invitation.

On the last days of November I lunched at the guide-post "Holyhead 194 miles," where an English robin, in size between a sparrow and a wren, with little crimson breast, hopped off with some bread crumbs. In December I still found abundance of blackberries in the hedge, with no one picking them but myself and the birds. I soon found big mountains crossing my path long before I crossed the frontier into Wales, with Rodney's Pillar on one of these, where once lived the bandit who thrived by overturning and robbing mail-coaches, whose horse had been shod with the shoes set backward, causing his pursuers to end up where he began!

IN THE WILD MOUNTAINS OF WALES

This is the cloud-wrapped mountain land,
Jammed with sights and scenery grand;
These are the people I love to know,
With hearts of fervor and pure as snow,
Modest, but mighty Wales.
—Lines in Welsh lady's album by Author.

I was in the land of the King of the Cymri, where the savage Picts lived in wanton sexual freedom. Protected by cavern barrier and dashing mountain stream, they long resisted the gentle rose-water and facial cream of civilization, when the Norman Conquest finally smoothed out the racial wrinkles of roving clans and softened the craggy features of petty kingdoms until after five hundred years of beauty-shop treatment, Wales has evolved. The Welsh are as different as are the Irish, English or Scotch. They speak in high-pitched tones, thinly nervous, and their songs are not rag-time. The language is even stranger than the race. Boot is esgid; crow is bran; dogs, cun; geese, gwyddow; cows, guartheg; men, dynion; women, cjwrogedd and sock, hosan. The cultivated Welsh lady speaks English usually, and has a voice of peculiar charm. The girls talk sweetly, —but what girl doesn't! Between landlord and tenant was a wide cleavage. English and Welsh were taught in the schools, and this common knowledge of two languages was bringing the two classes together. Children, ten years old did as good work in "Drawing" as do our pupils at the age of twelve or fourteen. The teacher stood behind the high desk all day long in these rude schools, where every pupil was mentally standing, too. Rugged in theology, the Methodist doctrine led. In the Sunday School the kiddies recited verses learned at home, as did also the young ladies, while the young men, as everywhere, looked on,—in a chapel furnished in fir-wood, with crimson cushions in a few of the pews, but with most of them hard and uncomfortable to sit in, purposely made so for the raw members who would have none of the "ungodly cushions invented by the devil."

The Welsh gave me less comforts but more cordiality than the English. There was usually a kitchen for the servants, a dining hall for the family, the male servants occupying the loft above the sheep-pen. At a farm near Llangollen that hung to a rocky hook on the side of the mountain above the River Dee, I was received with simple grace. Old but comfortable was the house, with hunting outfits hanging from the ceiling of heavy timber. Over a long table was spread the snowy cloth, with autumn and chill on the outside, when we sat down to mutton chops, milk, bread and butter, and the best blackberry pie I ever ate. You must go to Wales to eat mutton. In the poorer families I was served at six in the morning, bruised oatcake and buttermilk. At nine, bread and butter, with black tea. At noon, bacon and potatoes. At four, suran, a kind of soup. At eight, porridge, bread and butter.

For rugged beauty the Welsh mountains are a surprise. Geology points at you everywhere. Volcanic upheavals had squeezed the solid greenish-gray grit and slender bands of slate, limestone and conglomerate, with such force as to melt them into running streams of fire that on cooling left them with curvature of the spine, the several strata exposed in symmetrical flexion. In the valley of the River Dee lay great blocks of red limestone tumbled from sky-pierced crags as if glad to be rid of such mighty burdens. Usually gentle in outline, but massive in swell, they made easy wheeling on a polished path. Now you ride at their feet. The next two miles finds you half way up their noble heads, letting you look down, as you ascend, upon smiling valley of silvery azure, far, far below. Mellowed by the distance down, its glance is wooing. Ahead of you, and above you, are still higher peaks, luring you up from the sylvan charm. You ride out over trees tall, or soar far above them on a down-grade to another summit,—like a bird, with hollow bone, ball-bearings and rubber-tired. Now you turn abruptly to the right, then just as sharply to the left, amid thousands of vistas, so eager you can hardly wait to see what's next, but loathe to leave what is passing; spell-bound, you are their willing prisoner, glad to be hugged tight in their giant arms against their dewy cheeks, under their brawny brows.

Here comes a flock of sheep, with soft, long curling silken wool. They do not get out of the way. Now a-lead, now among them, now behind, the shepherd dog directs. Here comes a trap with two laughing girls, their horse nearly falling as he turns a sharp curve under a mammoth projecting boulder. High above, an eagle soars, about to perch on an eeyrie a thousand feet up. Far below, in a tortuous maze of glen, glides, now fast, now slow, a small boat of belated tourists down stream to the Glen Hotel. The picture is all but Alpine. Now we ascend again, only to descend, then up again, and wind around and around until the compass is agog, only to descend again, with brake applied. The air is the cool of autumn. It is health to be out. It is wealth to be a-go. Now we glide around the thirtieth curve, where falls away a winding flow of road with a thrill in every foot, where the danger from a broken fork or slipping brake adds to the uncertain joy, the wheel singing the song of full speed, musical in the soft melody of motion, each cavern, each clump of trees, each glen sounding its own echo, blending with the constant tintillation of the steel balls in their perfect bearings, merging in the far away whisper of the green valley below, composing a pastoral lay, never read on musician's staff. Still I go down, through overhanging trees, kissed by every-varying layers of scented air, warmer, then cooler, then warmer again, with clear water gurgling above, leaping into the very roadway to hide in a deep pool by the side of a great oval, red boulder, before it hies away and gushes over the cliffs, to dance down in a hundred little cascades that make it laugh, and cry, and pout. The soft music of falling waters among mountain boulders is the most soothing melody I know.

In a long valley that will soon take us to the foot of the main ascent, the wheel shoots across some old stone bridges, massive in rugged strength, weather-browned, spanning wild streams by Roman arch, gold and crimson ivy running rampant. Close by is the railroad viaduct, high and picturesque, over the Dee.

WITHOUT A CENT

Near by is the canal viaduct or bridge of water, begun by Telford in 1795, crossing one hundred and twenty feet above the stream, sustained by nineteen stone arches so slender they look too weak to bear up the flowing channel of water with heavy-laden boats. Seventy rods long, it impresses with the contrast of civilized genius and raw mountains wildness. Ruins of grand old castles leer on all sides, hanging right to the side of the perpendicular abyss.

The evening had been calm, the close of a perfect day. A group of peasant women, wearing queer broad-brimmed hats of mannish type, halting for a quick drink at a spring, hastened as if they knew by long experience in these mountains, the nature of the cumulous cloud now hanging over the peak, that was soon to break and roll down the ragged sides with darkness and tempest instant. In the hope of finding some mountain inn, I wormed up, dismounting on the steeper slopes, and pushing my wheel where the way was treacherous. Had I known of the desolate pass over the wildest of crags, and the long miles of dangers in a drenching rain among rock-locked chasms requiring daylight and trusty guides to cross, I should have turned back.

No one seemed to live up here. Not the sound of a living creature save the cry of a leopard or other wild animal could be heard, the darkness cut by forked lightning, the thunder with deafening tumult. My lamp was still burning, but the wind became so wild, the downpour so heavy, the rays seemed to blow back, unable to pierce the watery darkness ahead, with progress at times almost impossible, and the constant danger of being blown from the road. My tea of two slices of bread and butter had been too little for the energy now demanded. The higher I went the greater the force of the storm, and the farther off seemed the crest. Without knowing it, I had crossed the Pass, when my wheel, on the down slope seemed to drop out from under me and shoot forward in a weird manner, uninfluenced by the brake. Though the road seemed to rise in front of me, an illusion common at night, I found it running away, below me, at such a speed I was afraid to set the brake. The hills were of dark blue slate here, the same slate from which school-slates are made, their color and shape only intensifying the utter gloom. Above, in the crags, the wind howled; about me it swooped, with the wild fury of a maddened eagle, blowing me this way and that, twisting my cycle cape about my head and neck as it cracked the whip over my shoulders. Then a cruel blast took away my light where it was impossible to relight. On the right or wrong path, I knew not. I just kept on, desperate, my shoes full of cold water, until an overhanging portion of the mountain offered a cave-like shelter where I waited. The storm seemed to center its fury upon the defenseless peaks. From my safe position I could hear the rocks, washed loose from their moorings, tumbling to gullies far below, snapping off trees, and crunching the shrubbery in their course. The whole mountain side became a flood of hysteric water, sweeping the road with a force hard to resist, bearing driftwood and dumping it at the entrance to my shelter. Several streams, gathering from ravines above, poured over the knob under which I waited, carrying with them stones of great size that dropped intact, or smashed into pieces just outside of my cave. Though my feet and legs were wet, I found a dry match that lighted my lamp, which guided me from the cavern now leaking and threatening to fall in.

I have always had an instinctive fear of a body of water, particularly if suddenly discovered at night, a fear that impels me toward rather than from it. I had walked and ridden a short distance when the black outlines on my left gave way to a whitish stretch of surface far below. The flashes of lightning revealed it clearly, though more like a mirage than a real body of water, as it formed jagged bays under brow-beating cliffs. I moved cautiously to the edge of the wall, when a bolt of lightning struck near by, lighting the whole valley below and setting off the ominous peaks on the other side. Hugging close the very wall, here rising perpendicularly from a great depth, was the real body of water. As there was no sound of wave it could not be the Irish Channel, but river or lake, it was there. Its presence in the darkness gave me an uncanny feeling, and when I found that the wall of the roadway had been washed away a few paces on, I shuddered at the thought of my being hurled out from the road into that watery grave, for the road here turned off abruptly, hiding itself by its acute turn, while the break in the wall resembled the extension of the road.

The water basin soon narrowed to a stream. From the deep chasm I could hear the hoarse gutteral of falling floods, dozens of gullies pouring their burdens into the lake with deafening crash on one side, and with raging roar on another, while the very ground under me seemed to be slipping away with the racing tide that poured through my wheel and over the tops of my shoes, all but washing my feet from under me. Thrice out I lighted my lamp under the edge of a boulder, not far from which a ray from it revealed a hunter's cabin. The only response to my yelling and knocking was a series of mocking echoes. The lamp flickered and went out. Should I break the door down and enter this shelter, waiting until daylight to find my way to more comforts? Not even the owner, knowing of my condition, would possibly object if I paid him for the damages to the door. But I was too wet; and there was still a chance of my reaching human habitations.

As I went on the gorge gulched deeper and deeper as the mountain rivers tumbled with greater fury to its appalling depths, the incandescent glow of smashing spray throwing over the gloomy setting a feeble light that set off the hills of slate like grim spectres crouching before a smouldering camp-fire. By the aid of that light I rode forward on a better piece of road, though very steep and violent in curve. Again the wheel seemed to be getting from under me as I repeatedly saved myself by leaping from her on a road cut from the solid mountain wall. Several times I collided with the balustrade built up at the outer edge to prevent a fatal plunge, when the road turned abruptly from its advertised direction, scratching my leg on the outer edges and peeling my hand as I broke the force of the collision.

Then I saw some lights on my right, as I ran and rode, until I came to a settlement like a village, at the first prosperous house of which I knocked. A waiting maid carried my card, wet and limp, to her mistress, with my request for shelter for the night. Then a pretty young woman came to the door at once.

"Come in and take a seat by the fire," she said, sympathetically.

While drying my socks and wet clothing by a blazing hearth, she gave orders to her maids in the kitchen. Big pieces of bacon hung from the ceiling amid sage and vegetables. Yet there was an air of respectability and comfort about the house suggesting hospitality out of the ordinary awaiting me. Now and again she would come and speak to me, each time letting me be more assured that I was not only to stay all night, but that I was greatly welcome. Peat cut to the size of bricks burned on the open fireplace. On the mantle was a set of copper kettles. On the fire-hook hung an iron kettle covered by an iron lid, the steam issuing from the pug spout near the top. Fire-tongs and toasting forks lay to one side, propped against the fender. In a side room on a long home-made table male and female servants were setting dishes and food, in the center of which were silver coffee and tea pots with china cups. Supper, the last meal of the day, was all but ready, for it was nine o'clock and not midnight, as I partly expected. I was putting on my shoes when my gentle host came again.

"I have invited a few of my girl friends to take tea with me tonight," she said. "Won't you step in and take some with them?"

GREAT GLIBBERGEFITZ!! Not "you may," but "won't you?" So she took me, not to the table of the servants in the kitchen, but down into another room—the guest room, two steps down—where was a second hearth all aglow. At the steaming table, with flowers at both ends, she presented me to four girls of high-school and college age!! Out of the darkness and danger I had come into a young man's greatest chance—five impressionable females of cultured training and winning graces—to talk with them over English tea, Welsh lamb, Irish butter, Scotch meal and American need!

Then the girls sang at the piano or listened to my adventure until a late hour. They were surprised that I made the Pass during the night and storm, where they told me of a cycling tourist who, while coasting the road, had met his death in daylight. Next morning (Sunday) breakfast was served me in bed. After luncheon of mutton roast, vegetables and pudding, the girls having stayed over, I went back to see by day what I couldn't see the night before. The cyclist ahead of me had been killed at the third and lowest curve of the three curves near the third mile-stone from Bethesda, fifty yards back from which I had dismounted at the going out of my light. Far below the road was the "Devil's Kitchen," where Idwal was cast from the top of the cliff, two thousand feet above. A little farther back I found the strange body of water, the enclosing mountain weirdly gashed with ragged rents, from the wounds of which still spouted forth foaming cataracts. There was also the "Devil's Punch Bowl," amid grewsome rocks, where even in daylight their uncanny shape and size made a fitting abode for the damned.

AROUND THE WORLD

Monday morning I rode away from the "Tyn-y-maes" farm, managed by a brother and sister, catching the little boat for Dublin, landing in a few hours at the North Wall, where on the very next voyage, after beating hopelessly through a violent storm, it sank in the harbor with fifteen passengers aboard.

THE LAND OF THE SHAMROCK

"O sunny isle of blooming woods!"

I took the whole winter to ride completely around the island, enjoying the hospitality of the kindest people on the globe. Up till New Year's I picked blackberries from the hedgerows. Although it rained three times a day and five at night, the weather was pleasant. The Irish jaunting car was the most striking difference here besides the people themselves. This buggy rides above the two wheels like a hen squatting over her chicks, the driver facing one side of the road and you the other. I wanted to strike up an acquaintance with my driver, so I told him I used to have an Irish neighbor by the name of "Rock."

"Well!" said he, "that's a hard name!"

I rode through Sackville street, the Broadway of Dublin, wide and straight, at one end graced by the Nelson Pillar and at the other by O'Connell's Bridge, going to the Bank of Ireland, not to draw funds, but to see its grand portico supported by four Doric pillars with giant sculptures on the tympanum, representing the union of England with Ireland, the figure seated on a shell, while Neptune drives away Famine and Despair. Sixty stupendous pillars as big around as hogsheads, thirty or so feet high, swing in magnificent curve.

Having been warned about the difficulty of making my way over Ireland, I was agreeably surprised on a ride north to Dundalk and return—such delightful country, with periwinkles growing in the woods and cabbage in the gardens, the grass as green as grass can be. The country homes were damp, and the fire-

WITHOUT A CENT

place sent ninety per cent of the heat up the chimney. I stopped over night in the Presbyterian manse with Rev. Harrison's family, being most kindly cared for in a richly furnished bedroom, where between the white merinos I fear I left a committee of "graybacks" or "cooties," which I had caught in some lodging-house before entering Ireland. In the morning my shoes had been cleaned and polished, and when I left this dear man put into my hands a silver florin.

About ninety per cent of the natives are Catholics, while most of the ten per cent of Protestants live in Belfast and the North. I was cautioned not to mention religion in my talks, and when I taught some of the children to sing "Precious Jewels" the police informed me I had better desist. On Christmas day I stopped in a little town where my home was with a family who kept a little grocery in the front or living room, while my bedroom was just off the rear. Hastily entering my room that evening in the dark, I was struck on the hands by something like a ball-bat. Striking a match, I found the donkey, with head down and heels aimed for my nose, ready for a second trial at me. The chickens sometimes came into my room, too, but as a rule they roosted on barrels and boxes or on the scale beams in the grocery. In most homes the floor is constantly wet from rain coming down the big chimney and by waste water being thrown there, the floor often being of loosely laid brick or the ground. Over this the rosk-cheeked baby crawls to rugged health.

One noon I stopped at a prosperous farmer's house, where a shyly modest girl of seventeen received me in the hall, where her tall father invited me in to a place made for me at the table between the two tall sons. When I saw that I had been put into the chair occupied by the daughter I refused it, but they made me keep it. Long slabs of bacon hung from the ceiling near the fire-place, some of which was on the table

AROUND THE WORLD

stewed with cabbage and spuds. Again and again the farmer helped me to the pork, sweet and tender, while the girl brought me a pitcher of rich milk and a plate of yellow butter, after which she passed the bread she had baked. The Irish loaf is round and flat, about the size of a baby-carriage wheel, usually made of buttermilk. It is good, but no amount of butter makes it taste like other bread. The two boys were as shy as their sister, and both left the table with plates half-emptied.

Arrested

In a little town I asked for lodging and was directed to a plain plastered house that proved to be the home of one of the cops. He "marked" me instantly and went out, to return in a short time with another cop, both of whom looked suspiciously at me and quizzed me. When I left the house to get rid of them and to see the sights before dark, these men followed at a distance, and when I returned they asked me if I had come from Scotland. These two men and a third police found on the street gave me glances that upset my nerves. I had heard so much about religious persecution here, and as the town was thoroughly Catholic, I believed they meant to do me harm. All evening they stayed by me as I sat forlornly at the fireplace, watching me constantly. It was about nine when one of them left the house and returned shortly with a paper, saying as he asked me to stand up, "I arrest you as blankety blank from Scotland Yards." Just what Scotland Yards were I did not know at that time.

"Youse look loike a fair lad, but we nivver go by looks as fer 'ristin' a man," he said. "Show us your papers."

"You're all right, sir; right yez are," said the cop. "Without that you would be spendin' a night in the free lodgings."

Then they told me they had been looking for an insurance fraud escaped from Scotland.

IRELAND

Irish Constabulary

Irish Cart

IRELAND

Three Hundred Feet Above the Ocean

Where Author Met the Real Irish

WITHOUT A CENT

That was in the north of Ireland. In the south of Ireland I had more trouble. The south is bitterly opposed to the English. Wexford is a city in the south. In its market square one Saturday night I gathered a mob about me and began. In the north I had been taken for a Scotch insurance fake. Here the mob chased me down a back street because they thought I was an Englishman. I felt humiliated at what had happened, and next morning I had a notion to remain indoors all day. But it was New Year's Sunday. I changed my mind and went to the Methodist Church. After the sermon a tall man introduced himself to me as the justice of the peace. He said he happened to be passing the night before and saw the mob. So I began to be sorry I had come out to church. Then he invited me to go with him. So I more than half expected to be arrested again. We walked to the edge of town and then up to a high wall and to a big stone house setting well back in the center of a great lawn. It was his own palatial home. In the big drawing-room he introduced me to his family as we sat down to turkey and cranberry sauce, and the next morning he presented me with one of his most beautiful—no, not daughters, of which he had three of school-age—but pieces of gold to help me over the island.

In Waterford the temperance folk had me remain with them for several weeks while preparing a two-night show. The committee asked me to distribute advertising matter concerning it to which I seriously objected, saying that in America it would be suicide for a lecturer or entertainer to show himself much before his appearance on the platform. So, trusting to their judgment, I went all over town. When I stepped on the platform none needed an introduction. We had run against each other a thousand times. But it was a critical audience, so I felt my way along, as I did in the Welsh mountains, until they gave me implicit trust and applause the most sincere. From that moment we fell in love with each other and, like a lover, I could not do too much for them. There was complete fusion of speaker and audience, and I could feel the pleasure of the invisible currents of magnetic control.

In the history of Christianity no form of its development has elicited such marked and thrilling interest as the study of monasticism. In it reposed the science and art, the culture and hope of the world. After a hard climb up a long mountain I came to Mount Melloray Monastery, shutting in from the world the Trappist Monks of the Cistercian Order of France, to be shut in here myself for five days.

"Go in there," said the Prior, meeting me at the gate, habited in a long white and black robe with cowl drawn over his head. "It'll be a fine place for you to rest." Another monk greeted me kindly and showed me where I might keep my wheel, when I met the Guest-Master, who received me with a warm handshake. It was funny to shake hands with these old monks of five hundred to a thousand years ago. I thought they were all dead!

"This will be your room," said the Master. "Dinner will be ready soon. You will hear the bell."

Assigned a seat at the table, the Master said, "You can now eat of our plain meal." Grace was said by a visiting priest from Scotland over big joints of roast-mutton and pork, boiled potatoes, cabbage and several kinds of bread. I declined ale and stout and took water instead. Everything on the table had been produced by these monks right there on the mountain side. While we ate one of the monks read to us from "Meditations," as the monks served, coming and going in modest silence, like a poem in harmony.

"We get nothing," said the monk when I asked him as to salary. "We havn't need for a single penny. Every one has an object in view," said he, "but ours reaches to Heaven," quoting, "He that looseth his life

WITHOUT A CENT

for my sake shall find it." On the walls was the word SILENCE!

We were shown the hard plank beds on which these monks must sleep, and from which they arise every morning at two to pray in the chapel. I broke a rule of my own here, that of tipping, and gladly dropped a gold coin into the "poor box" when ready to say good-bye and coast down the mountain on the other side by the charming Blackwater, deeply fringed with woodland greens of ivy, ferns and summer foliage, where at a grand sweep of the river the old bridge comes into view, beyond which is Lismore Castle, where I saw the famous Bishop's crozier of 1113. I looked out of the window where King James once stood when he grew dizzy as he looked so far down upon the flowing water. The surprise to the king, as to me, was the great contrast in the two levels outside —the front being approached by a fine sward of grass from a much higher level, while the river falls away precipitously to a great depth, with the wall of the palace built right up from the water. The view of the river here and of the Knock-me-all-down Mountains is one of the most charming in Ireland, if not of the world.

The Good Templars of Cork advertised me for "Two Nights Only" as THE GREAT AMERICAN ORATOR! on posters four feet high. As I had not at that time been known as a platform attraction, this publicity to my school-boy ambitions, petted my vanity. They gave me the entire proceeds of my two lectures and paid all of the expenses out of their own pocket. I had a room by the famous Shandon Bells, where I read my home papers, scanning my travel letters in them with queer interest. After a good letter from one you love, the home paper brings the greatest joy. The news items told me of great changes reconstructing the old familiar map of life to which I as a youth believed I was bound forever. Not only the traveler, but all of us are Rip Van Winkles, com-

AROUND THE WORLD

ing back to our childhood's home to find, with sinking heart, little trace of old-time scenes, to meet no more many of our playmates we have loved or hated, and for whose admiration we have striven.

> "There is a stone there that whoever kisses
> Oh he never misses to grow eloquent.
> 'Tis he may win a maiden's love,
> Or become a member of Parliament."

Of all daring feats, delivering an oration before a college faculty not excepted, this was the most hazardous of my life. When I had climbed the old stone stairway up the dark tower I found the Blarney Stone built out into the parapet wall several feet and down from the castle top on which I was standing. Just to look down through the wind-gutted opening, one hundred and twenty feet from the ground below, made me tremble. Several times I changed my mind, overcome by fear, gladly assuming that such a heroic venture was for greater heroes than I. If I kissed it I would have to let myself down to it, head first. The tourist who went the other way never got back. Then I ran down and begged the Irish girl selling curios to come up and hold me while I did the kissing. She blushed and said, "I'm afraid, mister, I can't hold you tight enough." Back I went, determined to do it or die. Most tourists use a rope or have their feet held by friends, the latter very uncertain and unduly risky. I removed my coat and vest. On these I laid my cap. Then I crawled out over the abyss. I looked down on the top of a tall pine just below. Then I got up and ran down to the girl again, urging her to come up and help me. "You better not, mister," she pleaded; "no one risks it alone."

Back up I flew. This time I kept on my coat and pulled down my cap—to break the fall if I did go down. Then I prayed. Crawling to the edge, I seized the two vertical iron bars running down and support-

WITHOUT A CENT

ing the stone, and began to slowly descend, hand under hand, the iron, cold and slippery. But if either hand slipped the least mite it meant a plunge head first to certain death. My knees had now reached the edge of the rock floor. An inch farther would place the entire weight of my body on my hands. Inch by inch I descended, my head and shoulders wedged against the parapet wall that hung so far out from the platform on which I lay, and was now slipping from, that my feet only now clung desperately to it. My life depended upon my hands. Almost the entire weight of my body was on them. If one of them should become paralyzed! My eyes were staring at the Stone, but still I couldn't help seeing the one hundred and twenty feet of space below me, and the rough rocks I would fall on, if I suddenly lost my strength or nerve. But the Blarney Stone was still two feet from me, out and down. Slowly, and more slowly, I wormed down and out, and still down, and then a little more, and a little more, my hands trembling and my muscles tiring, until I had gone down so far I knew I could not get back—not unless I succeeded in kissing the Stone, and using it as a help by which to push my body up and back. The wind whistled up through the opening, adding terror to my position, my hands chilling and numbing. I was at the end of my reach. If I slipped but an inch, the only way out would be down—a hundred and twenty feet!

But I was still up there and hanging on. I knew now that if I did not kiss it I could not summon enough strength to get back, for failure robs of strength as well as of skill. My mind became as clear as a diamond. I was living the Nth power, when seconds were hours. Then I became hysterically happy. I was still up there, alive and safe, and I believed I could do it. Right there before me was the Stone. My forehead pressed it, but my lips were six inches away. In another ten seconds I would fall, anyway. I knew that. So I used the last remaining strength in twisting my head around, my weight upon my outstretched arms, then screwed my face around, raised my head back, puckered out my lips and let my body swing against the right spot, planting a truly impassioned kiss right where it ought to go! Gripping still tighter with my last ebbing force, and using the outer wall and the Stone as an impact, I pushed up and back, and on and up, until my knees had worked back over the edge above, when my cramped muscles, relieved of much of their burden, worked on faithfully until they had me safe again on top of the tower.

Laughing and crying for joy, I leaped to my feet, danced around the top and looked down over the parapet to see if I could find someone to tell my good news. An Irishman was approaching. To him I tossed penny after penny, telling him I had just kissed the Stone—I had to tell somebody.

From Coachford the mountain-path crosses the Glashogariff into a little town with a big name, Carrigadrobid, on the lazy Lee, with a charming old castle, rivaling the Rhine, rising amidstream as a buttress to the bridge, the site chosen by the beautiful Una O'Carroll, whose infatuated lover built the castle-home to satisfy her queer whim. Leaving Inchigeelah, the Carrynacurra Castle browbeats the cyclist from a rugged escarpment near the mystic lake of Gougenabarra, walled in by precipitous peaks eighteen hundred feet above it, and reflecting their gloomy silhouettes in the clear water hugging their feet in fear. In the center of this haunted lake, which is about two miles around, rises the miniature island known as St. Finn Barre's retreat, now in ruins. Not caring to be caught here at night, where "ghosts walk," my wheel coasted roads as smooth as glass on a down-grade that took my breath, mile after mile, as I drank the air-like liquid lemonade, into the Keinabeaigh Pass, "where the severed rocks resemble fragments of a frozen sea." Then for a mile I ascended, the Pass narrowing until just wide enough for a wagon, the giant walls rising almost vertically until the very summit is reached, when scenery really begins!

Here I began a long descent to Bantry Bay, tropical in its climate, where lungs and throat are ever healed. At the summit of "Sugar Loaf" I snapped a little girl who brought me a glass of milk as sweet as the spring laughing its way out from the deep brown rocks. She refused pay for it, and so I will honor God's little steward by preserving her in this book. Riding the cool tunnel I began an eighteen-mile coast, the longest around the world save one in the Alps. Flying so fast through this wild scenery I had to look quick as things shot past me. Panorama after panorama, near and far, on both sides of the perfect road unrolled. I was in Kenmare before I thought I was half way there! I want to ride this road a hundred times—this masterpiece of divine glory, adorned by man's epic in roads!

Gold and silver clouds floated the afternoon sky as I climbed a new range for my first glimpse of Killarney. Riding leisurely through Windy Gap, the road took an abrupt jerk to the right, then a sudden drop, showing in the deep purple valley of M'Gillicuddy's Reeks a conceited little lake vainly trying to make me believe it was Killarney. By suggestive look of mountain and atmosphere ahead, I knew that something more wonderful than anything I had seen was about to be revealed. The rosy atmosphere crowned a layer in purple mists that shimmered in cloud-shadowed sunshine of summit and slope, the lower levels deepening in darker purples, half-hidden under the gauze of approaching night. With cap in hand I was riding another ascent, and still another, when with evening sun on my back, my breath held in, lo! the three magic lakes, like jewels on a silver cord, burst suddenly into view! The air was still. Mellow music creeped up from the valley as I drank in the fairest vision human eyes may gaze upon. "From here on," said my guide-book, "for eight miles the scene is as from fairy-land."

The drop became steeper and steeper, the scenery unrolling in magic grandeur. God made but one Ireland and one Killarney! Majestic in rugged beauty, this wild roadway, full of raptures, dazes the senses as in hypnotic trance. Evening in softest tints, evening in mauve and azure, lowered her modest curtain o'er the hills. The lakes, drawing the cover of semi-darkness about them, glistened in their soft beds as if lighted from within. Twilight, with her companion stars, set the full moon just over the lower lake as I rode up to Muckross Castle right on the bank and clanged the knocker at the gate.

A servant carried my card up, and I was admitted into the presence of Lord Clonmel and his two friends from London. I was to lodge at the High Keeper's place. When the family retired to the floor above, I bolted my door and laid down to sleep. But the night was too fine; the moonlight scenery was too inviting.

As soon as I believed the people were all asleep I arose, unbolted my door and stole out into the night. Dogs that had been barking earlier in the evening were now as quiet as the night. Never before had I seen such a wonderland of beauty in such a wonderful night. The full moon and stars acted like electric bulbs in the dome of Heaven. Not a leaf stirred. The silence itself was a symphony. The winter night was like June. And the light! You could read by it. Quietly I made my way past the castle and out along the main lake, getting farther and farther away from my host, thence into the mountain thicket, until the silence became more and more broken by the distant rushing of a waterfall from steep cliffs into its cradle of the lake. Birds, as much awakened by the bright night as by the rarity of footsteps at this time, fluttered among green-bowered trees, or with a few rebuking notes flew off to another leafy bed.

So eager was I on this night quest amid the wilds, I had not thought of fear from animal or man until the sound of footsteps a hundred paces ahead made me suddenly aware of the audacious risk I was taking alone in this rough region. I stopped and held my breath as I listened. Evidently I had been discovered first, for the footsteps as of one approaching ceased. But they began again, more definite and more rapid, hurrying as if to meet me. Then I recalled the strict police watch over Ireland. This was perhaps none other than a night patrol around the lakes or from the wild-deer region above them. If so, and I were discovered by him at this time of night, I would be arrested, for it was now after midnight. My credentials—but they were back on my wheel in the keeper's house. If he found me he might be willing to go back with me, call up the keeper and confirm my story, if indeed his "beat" reached that far. But the fact that I had stolen from his house after he had put me to bed as his guest might not be the easiest thing to explain to the keeper, especially when roused from slumber. So I meant to hide myself from the approaching steps.

The dense shade of a tree came almost to my feet. Into this covert I glided noiselessly and waited. For ten or fifteen minutes I stood here perfectly still, expecting every moment to see a dark form emerge from the thicket ahead. Now regular and now irregular came the sound, not so much like footsteps as I had at first believed, but more like a biting or chewing of some animal at the trunk of a tree. My heart beat more calm, for I confess that while I did not want to meet with any wild animals, I was more willing to take my chances with the worst kind of one rather than to be led back under arrest to the high keeper. But whatever it was, I turned back to retrace my steps to the lodge. After going back a short distance I reproved myself for cowardice and turned again to seek out the cause of the noise. Nearer and nearer I stealthily made my way through the tangled brush and heavy timber until I reached an open space on the other side of which was a clump of small trees near a rocky ravine. I knew that the object of my search was in that bunch of trees, so I tip-toed across the open space and then threaded through the shrubbery. Suddenly the noise ceased. My heart thumped. I was close to it, whatever it was. Then it began again and I took several steps nearer, as I held back the tangled branches with both hands and peered into the shadows. There it was, this thing that was making this noise that sounded like footsteps, a four-legged animal the size of a cow, with head from me and hind feet not over six feet away! It was chewing at the outcropping roots and bark of a little tree. Then I saw that it was a wild deer—the first I remembered seeing—in the act of taking its breakfast. How I had ever been able to get so near it, with instinct and sense of smell so strong, and to remain close to it I cannot understand. It seemed unfair that I should take advantage of the animal's sense of smell, hearing and sight, so I yelled, expecting it to take instant flight. To my surprise it remained perfectly motionless, ceased chewing, raised its beautiful antlered head and looked slowly and leisurely around without a single movement of any other part of the body and without a tremor of muscle. Then with sudden bound this giant stag shot away into the denser foliage up the mountain side, leaping the gully as my hair stood on end, covering rock after rock, his head raised, his antlers back, lying upon his graceful neck as he rocked in the full poetry of motion. For a minute I must have stood there looking in the direction he had taken, then at the spot in which he had just been standing.

Glad that I had conquered my fear and discovered the cause, I returned to the lodge and a little after six entered my bedroom, the family still asleep, the

IRELAND AND SCOTLAND

Belfast Ship Building

Bonny Scotland

IRELAND AND SCOTLAND

Rails Depressed in Scotland for Safety

castle quiet. I bolted the door and slept soundly until eight, when I was called up to porridge and venison. Only the stag knew of my night's prowl.

The next morning, like the night, was a perfect calm without a cloud. "If only you have a pretty day for Killarney," said my hosts along the way. And I did —"the finest in ninety days," the castle-folks declared. The grass sparkled in gleaming dew with wild flowers abloom. Contrasting with the smooth, clear water of the lake, the towering mountains, rising in dark masses, increased its limpid glow. A purple haze hung near their tops through which sunshine streamed like silken snow, the water of as many tints as the direction viewed, from the most brilliant flash that softened into mellow tints of azure, blues and greens, reflected by sky and hill. The sculling of a boat on the opposite side stirred the glassy sea into a million curls, the dipping of the oar a mile or more away was distinctly heard, while the pebble dropped by the girl from the stern sent circle after circle back that softly broke into the V-shape ripples of the boat and spread fantastic etchery behind.

At ten I sought the butler at the castle and saw through the vast kitchens. Here the "scullions" were at work, just as I read of them in historic novels—young and old, male and female—washing dishes, scouring pans, pressing clothes, packing hunting-outfits, uncorking fizz bottles. Talking and laughing at their duties, they were getting more fun out of their work than the lord got out of all his leisure.

ON THE BANKS OF BONNIE DOON

I landed in beautiful Glasgow from a little launch and made my home at the sumptuous Y. M. C. A. and the Model Lodging House, the Scotch introducing me as "Our very distinguished visitor," and learning by living with them their utter sincerity and goodness of heart. I had done the Scottish lake region on one of the finest of tallyho rides with a lot of Americans—swimming in the lakes and gathering heather, where

> "The heathcock shrilly crew,
> And morning dawned on Ben Benue."

On this bike trip to Scotland I could not rise to the wonderful heights of that first visit during a college vacation, but I was glad to be there again, for I longed to find a little lassie met at the home of Robbie Burns at that time.

So with the gentle breeze of spring kissing my cheek I rode into the Burns country through Ayr and stood on the banks of the stream where Robbie and his Highland Mary plighted their troth; walked into the field where he ploughed up the mouse, and into the meadow where he plucked the daisy, where I picked one for mother and sister; laid on his wall-bed in the old cottage; then rode towards the Bonnie Doon, near which lived the little eleven-year-old lassie whose snapshot of her and her chum, with signatures, I mixed at the time, forgetting which was "Jessie" and which "Linnie." Then in writing post-cards to them, what I said to one I was meaning to say to the other, and the one to whom I said the nice things did not seem to care, while the other to whom I was indifferent responded with enthusiasm. So when I located "Jessie" and called upon her, not far from Ayr, I was disappointed. She was not at all like the girl I had remembered. But she knew where "Linnie" lived.

"You gae the rood by the kirk in the vale, keeping the valley to the Doon. She lives in the stone-hoose amang the trees," she told me, seeming also to know of the mistake I had made.

How I did ride! Passing some houses plastered and whitewashed, I came to the kirk on my right, then into a flowery dell by the rapid-flowing Doon to a stone cottage behind shrubs and flowers. I banged the knocker several times, when a fine looking mother let me tell her who I was and why I had come.

WITHOUT A CENT

"O mon!" said she, "and are you the tourist from America my Linnie told me she met with at Robbie's hame some years ago?"

"Where is she?" I asked, impatiently. "Does she live here, and are you her mother?"

"Yes, mon! but come on in. Have a sate on a cheer. We'll be havin' tay soon. I dinna ken where Lin is."

"Don't say you don't know. I just came from her friend Jessie's and I must ride on. It will soon be night."

"You're in Scotland noo; it won't hurt you to get acquainted with us Scotch. We're canny folk on the bark, but we share the last drap when we ken you," and she went to look for Linnie. Though the house was small, it was built to accommodate a big family, where strength and beauty harmonized with neatness and simple thrift.

"Lin's in the glade after daisies. She'll be in any minute. I wouldn't wonder she'll be glad to see you." I was telling the mother of my proposed trip to the southern point of England and then to France, when the opening and closing of the kitchen door told of her return. Fourteen now, taller and prettier than ever, her light brown hair falling in silky softness over her shoulders before and behind, she coyly entered, walking confidently yet timidly toward me, mute with girlish naivette, as she held out her little hand. Wide between the eyes, with very small mouth, her full-rounded face suggested tact and winning charm in a remarkable degree, magnetic and alluring. The pure glow of outdoor health was on her cheek in color and dimple, with a skin so fair it was transparent, and eyes as wonderful in their blue as the sky above her home. So young, so beautiful, so precocious, this second "Highland Mary" seemed too good to touch.

"Did you see Jessie?" she asked, with evident interest.

I then told her about the mistake, and how I was

beginning to fear of ever finding her, as she listened rather than talked. And after a frugal tea of wafer bread already thinly buttered, we went strolling along the Doone, picking wild flowers just as Robbie Burns used to do, and in the same spot, watching the birds build their nests, and listening to the melody of the flowing stream. Her mother had asked me to stop over night, and so I was secure in present happiness, losing no worries about the future. In fact, I lived here for three days in April, the May of Illinois, with the little girl who had exchanged post-cards with me, and who in the interim had won a valuable scholarship for best grades. One day we called upon the neighbors, and on Sunday went twice to the little kirk down the road, and once across the fields to another church, in the afternoon. On one of our hill-jaunts we came upon a little lamb about to perish, its mother lying nearby where she had been slain by dogs. It made me think of Sankey's "Ninety and Nine," composed near here in one of his meetings. Led by Linnie, I carried it to a farm-house, helping the owner to feed it for the first time by means of a bottle.

On the last evening some friends were invited in to dine. My seat at the table of guests and family of several girls and several brothers, was between Linnie and her father—Linnie was the baby, and always sat next to her father. At the end of the meal, before we left the table, the father gathered up any bits of beef on our several plates, and deposited it on the platter holding the original, a typical instance of Scotch thrift.

"Come on, Lin!" called her mother, the next morning, as I was about to go, "and say good-bye."

She was only a school-girl, of course. I knew, on parting from her, that if I were ever to see her again, it would be only after I had completed my ride around the world from her door; and so, when I said farewell to her, as she so tactfully went with me a little way over the hill, I kissed her, for the first time.

WITHOUT A CENT

RIDE FULL LENGTH OF ENGLAND

I crossed into England and rode the Lake District. It was just after Easter, and hundreds of cyclists enjoyed the fine weather and roads. The scenery around the lakes was superb. The road hugs the base of the mountain covered with snow near their tops, while quaint country homes and splendid trees fringe the enchantment. Lying by each other, in humble graves, were Coleridge and Wordsworth, near Windemere, where I rode sixteen miles and back before breakfast, such easy riding were these perfect roads. The next day I rode one hundred and five miles, riding along the magnificent water system that carries the sparkling water through tunnels, over bridges, into a series of little lakes, each below the other, through a narrow valley, into Manchester.

My only puncture since leaving Ireland was when coasting the steep, long hill into New Haven, at the southern end of England, where I pushed it aboard the little Channel Boat at dusk, my cyclometer registered 5,225 miles.

IN THE LAND OF PARLEY VOUS

Not yet quite day when I landed, I found the road out of Dieppe on Sunday morning, May 3, breaking my custom of resting on the Sabbath. My first surprise on the French roads were the wayside shrines with life-size images of the Saviour on wooden, iron, or stone crosses, two to twenty feet high. Artistic, or rude and weatherworn, their presence made me feel safe. The next striking objects were the road-trees with clump of branches right at the tall top, with little beauty in their bare trunks, contrasting with the luxuriant trees of England. Then, too, the farmers lived in towns, and fields were not always defined by fences, while the dress of the men and boys around the stables was a loose overshirt reaching nearly to the knees. My first breakfast was of milk, white bread, and cold pork, in a little old plaster-house near a Catholic Church, where the children, parents, grand-mothers and bow-legged grand-daddies all came to worship at a service as uninteresting to me as to them, with no American hope or Yankee promise in their faces. Led by an officer in red and blue costume, with hat the shape of a boat, the priest marched up and down the aisles of the church, followed by singers bearing banners, with the entire congregation behind. The priest, a mild, sweet-tempered man, reminded me of the good bishop in Les Miserables.

Lazily I rode along country lanes past fields of wheat, vegetables and meadows. At twilight I emerged from a woodland into a fragrant valley where a wild doe shot across the road ahead of me, while I listened to my first nightingale singing its broken-hearted melody in the dip of the valley. Just as I climbed the hill on the other side, a flock of sparrows crossed above me, one of them striking the telephone wires and falling to the ground. Dismounting, I picked it up, as it died, in my hands, with a broken neck.

In a little town, over the hill, I was put under arrest.

Arrested and Tried

A crowd of loafers gathered about me where I had asked for a cheap lodging. Two officious men appeared who did not seem entirely satisfied with me. They tried to talk to me, but while I could read French easily, we were both so excited, we could not understand one another. I was about to get on my wheel, when the taller of the two men seized it, saying, "Come with us." With the two men on my left as questioners, I was given a seat behind a desk, the street mob now in front of it. I was in need of sleep, for I had slept none the night before, and my nerves were in no condition for the severe grill about to follow:

Q.—"Avez-vous des papiers delivere par le autorities civiles?" (Have you any papers delivered by the civil authorities?)

A.—"Oui. Mon Passport des Etats Unite. Vous—" (Yes. My United States Passport—you—)

Q.—"Pourquoi ne vous etes vous pas presents du

WITHOUT A CENT

consul Americaine?'' (Why did you not present yourself to the American Consul?)

I wondered how they knew I hadn't!

Q.—''Monsieur le maire croit vous demander de vouloir bien rester a sa disposition jusqu au moment on il aurait recu des ordres de l'autorite superieure. Que pensez-vous?'' (The mayor thinks he must demand that you remain at his disposition until he has received orders from the chief of police. What think you?)

A.—''Je vous monterai mon passeport si vous le desires; il est dans les baggages portes sur my bicyclette.'' (I will show you my Passport, if you desire to see it. It is in the luggage on my wheel.)

Then they asked me a question which I did not quite catch.

Q.—''Qu'est ce que ce vous dit?'' (What did you say?)

A.—''Ah-h! Pourquoi pronouncez vous bien le francais quand le voule vous?'' (Ah-h! How is it that you pronounce the French so well when you want to?'')

Q.—''Comment m'avez-vous pas d'argent?'' (How is it that you have no money?)

A.—''J'avais d'argent. Je ne pas parle j'avit ne pas d'argent. Je parlais 'parti Chicago sans argent.' Je partais san d'argent! Je coudrai logement. Je pense payer pour le meme. Permittre me partir.'' (I have money. I did not say I had no money. I said starting penniless from Chicago. I started without money. I wish lodging. I expect to pay for it. Let me go.)

I started for the door when the taller of the two men laid his hand on my wheel, and said:

''Non! Allons in le maison.'' (No! Go back into the house.)

A boy and girl pushed their way through the crowd to the table, leaning against it and looking into my eyes. When I needed strength to carry on my case I just looked into their sweet faces. They believed in me. So did I. I had seen the girl twice before as I entered the village, crossing the street with milk-pail, who responded politely to my salutation, with "Bon jour! Monsieur." An old lady, dusting the furniture about the room, looked at me as if she, too, knew I was innocent.

The smaller of the two men, who proved to be the school teacher, knew a little English.

"Allons! Suivez-vous nous." (Come, follow us.)

The two men seemed to disagree as we walked down the street. The taller man rapped loudly at a big gate. It was the mayor's home, the several women wearing white caps, all of whom were most kindly disposed to me.

Q.—Six arrestations have been opered and it is reserched two others men," was the reply of the teacher why I was detained, "because this gentleman have killed a policemen," he tried to tell me.

A.—So you thought I was a murderer?"

"So! So! You should have passport shown."

"You gave me no chance to get it. You suspicion the stranger too eager to show his credentials. Je suis mon passport! I travel on my face. I am my passport!"

My moment of freedom seemed near as they scanned my passport, and still more aided when the two children of the court-room entered the house, coming close to me—the mayor's own children! Their truer interpretation of character is only another lesson taught us of children who know innocence from villainy when their elders are often mistaken. While they looked over my passport I arose from my chair, drew aside the lapel of my coat, and revealed there a little silk flag, the Stars and Stripes! pinned there the day I left, by a young woman, sixty years old, in Illinois.

"Arrest me if you please," said I, "gentlemen, when you trouble me you trouble my country, the United States of America. I am a native of Polo, Illinois, a citizen of that state, and I am pledged support and protection in every country to which I may come. In the morning I will cable to London, to my American Ambassador there, Extraordinary and Plenipotentiary, I shall not treat this affair lightly.''

The effect was electrical. They begged me to forget their undue haste, shook hands with me, and treated me as if I were the President! Then the mayor invited me to sup with him, and though it was ten o'clock, neither I nor the two little children were hungry. Their appetites, like mine, had been scared away.

The teacher then took me to his home. It was nine when he awoke me, the sun shining in my windows and the birds singing in the cherry blossoms. I followed him as he passed through one of the rooms filled with pupils at work, to the dining-room, where "dejeuner" was served by his wife as she ate with us—omelette, roast veal, bread, butter and coffee. At the close, he offered me the choice of chocolate, or wine. While sipping the bowl of rich, aromatic—chocolate! he handed me a fancy box of cigars from which I refused to draw any, after which his young wife, to get even with me, made me set my feet on one of her dining-room chairs, while she cleaned and polished my shoes with her own hands. When ready to go, the entire village came into the square to see me off.

At noon I took dinner at a farm-house in a landscape as gentle as my hosts, the soft colors of early growing things flecking the fertile soil. My wheel leaned against a great old beech that with several others, sheltered the humble home. Cut down now, or shot away by the enemy's shells, trenched and cratered, both home and hosts are gone! There were four in the family—father, mother, daughter of sixteen, and I. The cow shared the west end. Then came the kitchen, and next the bed-room. The food was passed around our little table, two by four, just as we always did at home, and we cut our own slices of bread—white bread from long, slender loaves, with vegetable soup, boiled potatoes, carrots, cabbage, pork, and a bitter beer which I only tasted. We sat close to each other at this little table, and no matter where the girl sat, I was close to her, any way—this French beauty with black, luxuriant hair, and wonderful, large eyes of some color or other that made me look long after I should have turned away. Polite and courteous, reverent and thoughtful, this family and others with whom I mingled, lived in their homes as in the presence of God. There was little furniture. The stove, shining black, was divided into three parts. Nearly as high as our own hard-coal stoves, the first part was round in shape, and held the pot, directly over the fire. Next was the middle portion with lid. The third part, round and bigger than the others, held the water in the reservoir.

Women worked in the fields with the men, hoeing, and driving horses or cows to queer cultivators. One farmer, mopping his brow, as he rested from pushing a hand-plough, looked like the "Man with a Hoe." "Not at all good," said he. "Man was not made to slave like this." I agreed with him, and told him that if he lived in the great Mississippi Valley he needn't push a plow. He could get on and ride!

IN LITTLE BELGIUM

The small fields were farmed right up to the fences, and there were no weeds. As in France, hardly a house stood alone in the country, and these were usually built of stone, brick or plaster. Dutch wind-mills were frequent. Horses, when used, were large, though in some parts these were a novelty, for dogs took their place— little dogs, big dogs, fat dogs, lean dogs, dogs friendly, and dogs savage, one, two and often five pulling at a wagon or at plows in the field. Sometimes a woman and dog, or a man and dog, pulled together. These dogs pulled tremendously hard at heavy loads. Some of the masters, inclined to be cruel, seemed to get no pleasure, but only profit out of the work. Four-wheeled wagon-loads of hay were pulled by several

WITHOUT A CENT

dogs at the front, several under, and still others behind the load, the ones under the wagon so hitched that if they hung back and failed to do their part, they were tortured by sharp prongs fixed in the right spot. I sought friendship with a big dog hitched to a milk wagon, but he thought I wanted to steal the milk, and leaped at me, nearly upsetting the wagon. On the Battlefield of Waterloo I snapped a wheel-barrow with a dog pulling at the front, and a woman pushing from behind. Near it a forest had been planted to take the place of natural woodlands becoming extinct.

Late one night I was shown my bed in a big room filled with others already asleep. My little candle lighted only my own needs, and I saw no others. I disrobed and crawled in. Next morning I was surprised to hear feminine voices in some of the beds around me. The double beds held married couples, while children and single folks, including bachelors, like myself, occupied cots. I was perplexed. I hardly knew whether to get up first, or last. I had no kimona. In neither France nor Belgium did I see evidence of social misconduct. The Belgians were less polite, but more sincere, than the French.

It is contrary to police rules for one to sleep in a straw-stack in Belgium. I meant to save my lodging expense the following night by sleeping out. About sunset I came to a fine straw-stack near the fence, but as there was a cop patroling nearby, I could not stop. A few miles ahead was another such stack of straw, but also another cop walking right by it. At the third one, the road was clear. I carried my wheel across the soft ground to this stack where a baling-press had been at work. So I used these bales to make my bed. I placed four of them in such a way so that I would have protection from anything save "Howling Berthas," and on the top of these I laid two more for a roof, crawling in just as rain began to fall. As my roof was about two feet thick, it was rainproof, but when the rain fell in torrents during the night, this cold water soaked under my bed. I was too energetic in turning over on my side, when the lower bales parted, letting the roof fall in upon me with such puddles of water as had collected on their spongy tops. When I became free, I built another bed, where, wrapped in my rubber cape, I fell asleep again, and when I awoke daylight had come.

Bread here was twice as high as in England, and bakeries carried but a small stock, as if it were precious. Sugar also was twice as high, with only a mite on hand.

INTO HOLLAND AT NIGHT

Saturday evening I rode out of little Belgium into Holland, and then on into the night. Monotonously level, with few trees, but acres of water everywhere. Canals were full of water, rivers full of water, lakes full of cold, wet water, the air full of foggy water that splashed into your face and ran down your back until you were soaked with water so that you never enjoy a drink in Holland. Water is around the hen-house, the well is running over, the pump is floating away, the cellars are cisterns.

The only interesting sight was thousands of Dutch wind-mills.

I rode all night, passing through scores of towns, in which a watchman stood on the main street, as guard. As he was expected to stop and inquire about everyone going through, I found it very annoying. So when I glimpsed them, as they waited my coming, I rode at them just as though I was about to run over them, turning my wheel sharply aside when close to them, and tramping my pedals, I was gone before they recovered consciousness. This was the only fun I had in Holland. Sunday morning I tried to sleep by a haystack in a town, where the water had frozen into ice. Holland is the mecca for skaters, where you can go anywhere on skates, even to bed. All forenoon families were afoot to and from church, wearing wooden shoes

WITHOUT A CENT

and sad expressions. At noon, one of these groups, a father, mother and a girl, turned into the plain country home. I turned in, too, and told them I would like to eat dinner with them if they would invite me as their guest. It was a treat to sit with the family in the big, bare kitchen, greater because I knew it would not last. The floor had been scrubbed with "Dutch Cleanser," as well as everything else, including the broom-handle. The only attraction was the way the girl "set" the rough-board table. She gave me a Dutch squint every time she went to the cupboard, and once she all but smiled. Black bread, hard and dry, little butter, some poor cheese, poor coffee, with sugar and milk, made the meal. Sallow and dark, the natives were rough in feature, with fewer pretty girls than in any other country.

I looked over my money and found I had English shillings, French francs, Holland guilders, German marks, and a few American coins. Computations in these monies was an education in itself, and I found it was unsafe to trust all foreigners in giving you the right change.

RIDING ALONG THE RHINE

I spent an hour in Cologne, going through the great Cathedral that took six hundred years to build, then riding directly to the Rhine road, dotted with passing steamers, the banks rising on both sides to mountainous heights, purple with vineyards and crowned by frowning old castles. The scenery was so wonderful I had no desire to stop when night came, but rode right on in the moonlight. It must have been two in the morning when I locked my wheel, and rested on a bench near a wayside inn high above the rapid river, the moon mixing purplish silver in the gurgling current that broke over a long series of rapids. Here I fell asleep, and was rudely awakened by a fellow who thrust a flash-light into my eyes. In the darkness I saw the form of another. I was asked a question in

German which I could not, or did not care to understand.

"Haben sie gelt!" (Have you any money?)

I thought it was none of his business whether I had any money, or not, but I didn't know what to answer. In Germany you are arrested when caught out like this at night with no money. In Chicago you are "held up" if you have it. If I said "No," and he were a police, he would arrest me. If I said "Yes," and he were a robber, he would take it! And that flash-light hurt my eyes, and biased my judgment, as I said, "Yaw-Nein!" (Yes-No) pretending not to understand his question. Then he went through my pockets, taking out every trinket and paper he could find. I acted as though I liked the idea of this midnight ruffian fumbling me over, and I helped him to find the many pockets I had with me. In one pocket I carried a wallet of three pounds English gold, a German sovereign, and some small coins saved up for boat-fare on the Mediterranean. Of course I didn't want him to get that. So I turned around, willingly, as he went through them, directing his movements, when at last we had been in every one save the "money pocket." So, when he was about to put his fingers into that one, I straightened up, as if to say: "How dare you hold me up like this? You've gone through my pockets once." And I pushed his hand away. Then I showed him my bicycle passport, talking rapidly to confuse him, at which he lifted his cap, and said:

"Gude Nacht, Mein Herr!" and was off.

Grabbing my wheel I dragged it along in the opposite direction, unlocking, and riding it rapidly away from the spot, fearing they might change their minds and come back, riding and walking until daylight, the panorama of the river increasing in gorgeous beauty at every turn. At the Lorely Hotel by the famous Falls sung about in Heine's lines:

"I know not whence comes this feeling
That I to sadness am so inclined."

WITHOUT A CENT

I had my breakfast—a hot drink of something called "schnapps," that by taste surely violated my temperance pledge—then coffee and bread. When these came I was asleep.

May and June had tumbled me from skies of blue into valleys of green. I rode up and down every hill along my way, over every stream—the Rhine, the Weser, the Oder, the Elbe, the Danube—and my lungs were bursting glad with fragrant air from red and blue and pink flowers, twenty acres of them in one field. I saw spring come over the mountains and laugh down the valleys and hug the hills, budding and bursting into flower and leaf, not in one country but in seven! I was in Ireland when the first petals began to color, then in Scotland in fuller bloom, then in England when the warmer blushes came thick and fast at the May-Pole Dance, to ride over France, Belgium and Holland, with spring at my heels. I was looking upon human custom and human face, natural beauty and endless scenery, the best I ever heard of, read of, or dreamed. My two thousand miles on the bike in Germany took me through Cologne, Coblentz, Mayence, Frankfort-on-Main, Hamburg, Marburg, Cassel, Goettingen, Eisleben, Halle, Leipsic, Wittenburg, Potsdam, Berlin, Dresden, Chemnitz, Nurenberg, Wurtenburg, Heidelberg, Karlsruhe, Strasburg and hundreds of towns. In the Hartz Mountains I sung:

>   Down the circling woodland road
>   My steed flies swift without a goad.
>   Merrily I glide,
>   In it confide,
>   And all I do is look and ride.

>   New-born leaves of freshness green
>   Add their pride to the sylvan scene.
>   I see two deer
>   Who inhabit here,
>   Start up and run with timid fear.

AROUND THE WORLD

Through the days of Springtime grand!
Deep in the woods of Allemand!
    My every day
    A holiday.
With me the woods for pastime play.

Of all tourists I got most out of my tour. On one side of the cherry-lined roadway I saw a woman hitched to a plow with her cow. On the other side of the road sixteen women and one man were hoeing side by side in a forty-acre field, while behind strode a man with a long-lashed whip. The only way to see these countries is by cycle or auto, the cycle being by far the best, and goes just fast enough for pleasure and profit. No other tourist had such fun as I. He enjoyed his wine and beer less than I liked my black-bread and spring water. He pretended to be rich. Everybody knew I was poor. People set but one foot to him—the best. I got both!

And how I coasted! Mile after mile, the rubber tires so soft and springy, flew without a flaw. While going at a terrific speed down a hazardous hill a gentle pressure on my New Departure put me in instant control. I had never seen those hills and I didn't know what was beyond. But while the rapidly passing scenery, unfolding in undulating panorama on each side, hill and valley opening to me their enchanting visions, desired me to pause, the more fascinating and bewitching wonderland ahead, half-hidden in the deep azure of the mountains, made my wheel take grade after grade as though it were a motor-car. So perfect the roadway, so gentle the swinging curve, so confident my wheel, I sat its back a master, my eye as calm as a placid brook. Tested so often, she became my confidante. Over her back I "threw the lines" and let her leap and plunge and sing for very joy, the breeze bruising my face as I shot through the artificial hurricane and up and around the other hill, so intoxicated with the delight of going

WITHOUT A CENT

fast that, like good wine, wants more as more is taken. The excitement of coasting a jumble of hills, with rapid glance of ever-changing scene about you and soft skies above you, with the wicked charm of shooting through and splitting the air in two—air thick with perfume—is the most delightfully exciting of all adventure. Mighty mountains melted into mole-hills, oceans became lakes, and as I shivered in the bed of forest leaves, the cold night rain dripping, the wolves barking, an irresistible purpose possessed me. I knew I would be victorious!

I rested in Luther's chair, sat in the window where he and his devoted wife used to make love after marriage as others court before. The last two days into Berlin I rode two hundred and twelve miles, the fastest of my tour, visiting several universities and other sights en route. Pushing my wheel down the streets of Berlin a man approached, who said that he was a London banker, and gave me a twenty-mark goldpiece, telling me to go to police headquarters and register, which I did, telling my name, origination, inclination and destination, a street number being given me where I could get lodging. I think he was a German spy, but the gold was all right. The next day I rode Unter den Linden, saw the Palace, the Art Gallery and the class-rooms of Von Humboldt, Schlermacher, Neander and Mommsen, where ten thousand students were finishing their education. I did not like flat Berlin and took the road again that same afternoon, making a bed at night in an artificial forest amid clumps of bushes so that I might be defended as I slept from an attack of animals roaming the wilds. There were no happy farm-houses along the way, for the farmers lived in towns. The next day I stood by the "Madonna," by Raphael, in Dresden, and at the lodging-house met a real one in flesh and blood—a poor working girl, whose exceeding fair skin and blue eyes attracted attention as she washed dishes or made the beds.

AROUND THE WORLD

I visited village schools as I rode along, in one of which the "lehrer" assured me he had seventy grades. After taking me through twenty of them he left me in charge while he went to market. I taught the class in "Reading," the boys and girls rising at their seat and reading to a period, when another would take the next sentence. I was helping a pretty girl in the penmanship class by putting my hand over her wee hand to help guide her pen, when the "lehrer" entered. These teachers were friends of the pupils, unlike the university professors, who entered the class-room with eyes at the ceiling, paying no attention to the students before them, either then or during the lecture. The pupils were very reverent, serious and obedient. On entering their room as a visitor they usually arose and repeated a verse of scripture, doing the same when I left them.

Locked Up for Refusing Drink

One rainy Saturday night I paid for lodging in advance at the only hotel in a village, and seated myself in the barroom, the only place provided for guests, where some youths were taking their social glass of beer. Wet from drizzly rain, depressed by hunger, homesick, I was in no condition for what was about to follow. Everywhere I was offered beer, but no one seemed to think I ever got hungry. So I lived on the plainest fare, black-bread usually being my only food on the road. Hotels in Germany were usually saloons, where every lodger is expected to contribute to the bar, men, women and little children drinking beer here, each with a big schooner before him, the babe at the breast having its sip at the mother's glass. That they might understand me, I showed the landlord my card introducing me as the long-distance rider around the world, telling him I was a temperance man, and could use alcohol only as medicine. But he was peeved. Then a young German set his own half glass down on the table before me, begging me to take sip after sip with him, after the German custom of friendliness. I tried to tell him why I could not taste it, thanking him. Puzzled at my German and bewildered at my refusal, he colored deeply, supposing he had offended. He called for a second glass and paid for it as the landlord set it down before me. Again I refused, trying to explain. The redness in the German's face increased. He ordered a third drink. Believing this were a temperance drink I raised it to my lips, but alas! the odor of alcohol! The poor fellow was in torment as he digged down for another and more valuable coin to pay for a third glass of something from a bottle high behind the bar—champagne, the best, used only for royalty.

The room was silent. The drinkers paused between swallows. All eyes were upon these glasses and me, The drinks looked so good, and I felt so bad, any one of them would have been good medicine to me, and by drinking one of them I might win back the landlord's favor, at whose mercy I was for meals and lodging. But I set the four glasses of drink away from me. In complete confusion the German gulped down the remaining beer in his own glass and staggered back to his fellows.

I had a desire to rush out into the night and rain and ride away. But I needed nourishment, and I would probably have been seized by the village cop just then looking in at the window. When ten o'clock came the landlord closed up, set my wheel behind the bar and called roughly to me:

"Commen sie!"

Thinking I was at last to have my supper, I hurried to him as he led the way through the milk-hall, where big pans of creamy milk were set upon the cement floor. Then through the kitchen he took me and out of the back door to the end of the walled yard to a sort of barn, where, opening the door, he pushed me in, saying I should sleep there, and closing the door and locking it before I knew where I was. I felt around a little in the darkness to assure myself I was not sharing my "room" with a billy-goat or a savage hund, finding a pile of hay on which I soon fell asleep.

In the morning it was still raining. It must have been about nine when I hammered at the door and called for my "jailer." Though I heard voices, no one came. About noon, assured of his intentions, I began to seek a way out. With a mattock hidden under some straw I pried off a plank and crawled through into another room, and from there to the next floor, where I took off another timber, and crawled into the chicken apartment. There was little commotion among the fowls, and I worked rapidly, soon having my head and one shoulder out through the small opening in the side of the barn used by them, from which a slender timber with slats at intervals ran to the ground. For some minutes I could not move either in or out, and the desperate effort to free myself sent the blood to my face and neck as I worked out and down to the ground. In the rain, without supper, breakfast or dinner, I rode away.

Many miles from here I hired out to a farmer in a village of one hundred houses and fourteen hundred people, near Neurenburg, at a mark a day. My room was over the cow-stable and pig-parlor. My cover was a fat featherbed that always rolled off before morning.

I was called up at four, to chore around, cut grass, and feed swine, with the hired girl. When the chores were nearly done she went to the house to get breakfast, and in a little while called out: "Kaffee Gekommen!" Then the hired boy would say to me: "Kaffee Gekommen, wir haben kaffee augenblick." At a little board table in this Gast-Haus we sat, while the family ate in the kitchen at a better table. Black coffee we got, with no sugar and less cream, and one solitary bun.

Then with hoes in our hands we went to the edge of town and hilled up hops that wound around tall stakes and over flat roofs of slender boards and wires. The

WITHOUT A CENT

men worked so fast I was tired in a few minutes, but they did not seem to notice it, and kept on as if racing. At nine-thirty one of the girls working with us went to the house and brought our second excuse for a meal—rye bread, salt pork, and seven schooners of beer. Beer never looked so tempting, but I refused it, and demanded milk instead, the men laughing at me, and saying: "Meelk ist fer pabies. Bee'er vill make du strength."

At twelve we went into the house for "mittagessen," with no knives or forks, but a wooden spoon to pour down the soup that was served in a wash-basin, with boiled spuds and rye bread. At four the first supper came—black bread, stink-cheese, six schooners of beer and one schooner of milk. My back ached and my hands blistered, but I hung on until sundown when we did the chores, and sat down to our fifth excuse for a meal—the wash-basin of camouflage soup—hot water in which red pepper had been thrown, and some stale rye bread floating around like gun-boats.

On the second day, while hoeing potatoes, the men worked more slowly, and before the end of the third, they fell behind me, as I was beginning to find my strength. I called to them to come on when they put me in the lead, and they seemed to think that the milk diet had triumphed. I was paid one dollar and forty-four cents as my wages for the entire week of sixteen-hour days and starvation meals.

A German Wedding

From the choir-loft in a village church, after a sermon for the occasion on the text: "Whatsoever he saith unto you, do it," I saw a wedding. The bride and groom, each on different sides of the church, seated with their respective friends, then arose, walked out to the center aisle, where they joined each other, and on reaching the pulpit knelt before it, the pastor joining their hands, when more scripture was read and a prayer offered. Then they walked down the aisle together, separating where they had met, each sitting apart, as before. A hymn was sung, and an offering taken, which amounted to seventy-five cents. Some cried. The entire marriage party then left the church, the groom with the men, the bride with the women, and all marched down the street to the bride's home, where they ate and drank all day and night, the pastor not present. His time came the next day when the bridal party surprised him at his own home with presents and money.

A German Funeral

I saw an impressive funeral of a little child, from a Catholic church, at about sunset of a beautiful day. Leading the procession were little children bearing the cross and banners, then came the little coffin on the head of a woman, followed by the priests, and behind these, men and women. The procession moved down a winding lane at the edge of town, and then by a narrow footpath leading through a tall rye field that bowed gracefully as they passed, to the cemetery, where three spades of dirt were thrown upon the grave by the priests and mourners, when water was sprinkled over the same and upon the people, after which every one left for their homes except the mother of the dead child, who stood alone by the grave and wept—just as the deep red sun sank into the calm fields.

Diary Jottings

German guide-posts, like American barber-poles, the name of town you are going to on the other side, so that you must look back after you pass it. Roofs of bright red tile everywhere. Postage stamps bought in one part of Germany not good in another. German universities overestimated. Drinking beer and duelling chief theme. Girls treated to schooner of beer at the bar after each dance, till three in the morning, when they are hugged at the door, each going home alone to avoid misconduct. No "courting" in Germany. When

GERMANY AND SWITZERLAND

Axenstrasse—Chambered Gallery

SWITZERLAND

lover calls he talks to her mother. Young people seldom ride together or walk together, unless impure. Berlin said to have more illegitimate children than Paris.

In the Black Forest

The grand prelude to Switzerland from Germany is the Schwartzwald or Black Forest, its entrance at the north being Biberach, where I spent the week-end in the Mayor's home, with three grown daughters and a son. Thrice elected as mayor of his town for a term of ten years each, I counted it an honor to spend some time in the presence of such a father. The first day I was told the time of meals. The next morning, Sunday, I slept late, and when I came down dishes had been put away, so I waited till noon. The father was head of the house, but needed not to say so. He came and went quietly, and read much. He seldom spoke. He had self-control.

Monday afternoon I began my last ride in Deutchland over roads prettier and smoother than boulevards, where queer, all-roof houses were hitched up to barns, and rested contentedly anywhere on the side of the hill, where water ripples everywhere in constant melody, every home having its water-wheel, always running, doing everything except bring the cows. Tryberg hangs on a silver peg of splashing water at the near top of a mountain you can hardly climb. The waterfall runs right down through the town at its own pleasure, generating a force that sets a trio of wheels running that turn the machinery for making the famous "cuckoo" clocks that imitate exactly the birds that I often heard as I rode along. Looking across from the waterfall the mountain express, like some magic monster, bursts suddenly from a tunnel and shoots among the dark pines like a hissing serpent, the eager tourists looking from windows as excited as you at the indescribable grandeur.

A little curly dog in this forest liked my idea of riding around the Globe, and left his master to join me, running by my wheel in great glee through several villages. He knew I liked dogs and understood them, for his soft round eyes took me into his confidence. To keep up, he ran at the top of his speed, but I knew it would be impossible for him to follow me all day on rapid rides. I frowned and scolded, but he still ran farther ahead, looking back to see me catching up. Then I threw him some food I carried, trying to slip away as he ate it. With beef and bread held in his mouth he caught up with me and ran on ahead of me. He was already miles from his home when I dismounted, caught him, started him backward, and threw a stone that struck and tripped him, hurting me more than it hurt my confiding friend, when he cried in pain, stopped short, and then, when I set out again, bounced after me, crying piteously to be taken along, when I threw another stone.

> Then back he ran and stopped and stayed,
> And looked with doggie's woe,
> While I rode on, a sadder man
> Than ere a dog could be.

WHEELING IN THE ALPS

The first thing you do in Switzerland is to arrive. You know at once you are here without being told. It is the spot where you always wanted to be. At Interlaken, the center from which to make many mountain climbs, I lived at the Grand Hotel des Alpes for three days, where mountain fountain sprayed in the sunlight over grass and flower, with glimpses of fairyland. When the polite Swiss waiter passes you the mountain honey you take more than you did the first time. The steak is juicier, the trout more snappy, than you ever tasted before, and you can eat a pound of their cheese at the end of your meal. The children on their way to a mountain picnic are prettier and neater than those of other European lands, and the drummer boy follows the Helvetian flag with a

WITHOUT A CENT

swagger only equalled by a doughboy behind the Stars and Stripes!

A glance through this idyllic beauty is awarded by a still richer panorama of green valleys and snow-kissed mountains. Every one admires Jungfrau, Queen of the Alps, visible from the Hotel, looking out upon the valley from behind surrounding peaks, shrinking away in modesty to reveal the chaste bosom and illuminated brow of their virgin queen to delighted thousands of adoring tourists gathered in nature's loveliest auditorium. Delicately draped in a thin veil of purple atmosphere, overhung and surrounded by Heaven's royal blue, the small but enchanting hills of emerald pose in the foreground that she may tower above them in all the splendor of bridal majesty.

In this enchanted nook I paused, with no business or social obligations to keep, my days of grace payable at sight in their own good coin. The girl I hoped to find might wait for me, or choose another. In Time's ripeness I would meet mine! Now I was here. Here, by the peasant's door, bright colored flowers bloomed. There blizzards broke in tangled fury and hurricanes prowled abroad.

Rivalling Interlaken is Lucerne, its first attraction the Lake, twenty-six miles long and a thousand feet deep, right on the beach of which it rests like a shimmering jewel. The next great sight is Mount Pilatus where I rested from my wheel by a ride on the cog railway, sleeping that night in a peasant's shack on the summit, that threatened, like the car, to pitch headlong down the mountain.

I rode the Axenstrasse, one of the finest roadways, as it hugs the lake and hangs from the mountain. On all sides rise the mountains, some naked, others dressed in pleasing green or shrouded in veils of mist and snow, with pride upon their lofty brows as they look down to see themselves pictured in the clear water at their feet, the wrinkles of their old age and

AROUND THE WORLD

the harsh ruggedness of their masculine might softened by the mellow illusion. Slowly we ascended this masterpiece of engineering cut from the solid granite walls pointing into the zenith. Ahead was the chambered gallery like a gorgeous box at Nature's theatre where we found shelter from a passing storm.

The road ascends very rapidly now, affording grander and more wonderful vistas. Half a mile from the Pass a snowfield blocked my way, while I cautiously advanced a foot, with all the terror of a possible snowslide started at any second by my own footsteps. At the very top a little auto bearing a honeymoon party from Algiers, met its Waterloo, and had to return to the Italian side. My way back to my wheel was not so easy as my way up. The snow by this time was melting, and under me were running streams that only Alpine climbers know how to fear, to fall through into any one of which meant certain death. I made great strides to my wheel, where on top of a big rock high and safe from the snow-field, I sung to an Alpine flower found nearby in the icy snow-water, as I took it to my heart:

To An Alpine Flower

Sweet flower,	Sweet flower,
That sweetly grows,	That silent blooms,
Here in the snow,	Here in the Alps
Unseen,	Alone;
I breathe with thee,	I dream by thee,
And breathing,	And dreaming,
Wish that I were thee,	Wish that I were thee,
In height,	In grace,
And place,	And form,
In this blue sky to live serene.	In silent majesty God's own.

There is more geology in one hundred square feet of Alps than a college text-book could hold. Millions of years ago these strata were laid down under water, then by earthquake, heat and pressure, were broken and bent, flattened, crunched in giant grip, once more to be petted back into life, for a million years or so, when the same demoniac fury again awoke as with one tremendous blast it smote these twisted layers of vari-colored rock, bore them aloft in Titan fist, whirled them about its shaggy head, destroying once more the animal and plant life it had invited into being. Here are the "folds," with "faults," "dykes," and "basins," "shears," "clines," "anticlines," "antisynclines," and "geosynclines," where the Leaves of the Book of Life are made, a million years apart!

Late at night I climbed the mountain opposite Simplon Pass, to study the next day the most thrilling of all glaciers—the Aletsch. Without waiting for breakfast I rushed out to take my first excited view of a real glacier at close view. On the other side of the valley rose the audacious Matterhorn, chilly white in cold chastity. Below, the flashing glacier, soon aglitter with diamonds in the flashing sun. I thought I could reach it in ten minutes, but it was miles rather than yards. I knew that glaciers moved, like a river, only much slower, about ten to twelve inches a day, and I confess I was afraid of it. It seemed to me that it was some terrible monster with self-consciousness, and I don't believe that anyone can view, from a good position, at close range, this or any other glacier without a unique experience in emotion. The air coming up from it is very cold. But when you get right up to it, and you actually see it move, growling and grumbling like a fettered giant, crushing great blocks of granite in its path, polishing the red sandstone of the mountain wall by unmeasured force of friction, and bearing on its back whole trainloads of rocks to be dumped at the Terminal Moraine, the melting water gurgling its frightful way down through gaping fissures, or flinging its greenish flood over precipice and peak—this solid stream of ice, miles in length, and hundreds and thousands of feet deep—you need the latest dictionary of words and ideas to help you tell a fractional part of your feelings.

What looked safe and smooth at a distance now revealed yawning chasms scaled only by ladders and ropes with strong guides. Tourists are tied together, about fifteen feet apart, to the same long rope, at the end of which is a Swiss guide with cool head and sure foot. Cigarette smokers are barred from these heights. A young smoker had been warned, but he persisted in being tied up with his companions. The two brave guides belted the rope around them, while two other tourists were tied in between them and the foolish fellow. As they neared the top, he grew dizzy on a ledge of rock, and before the guides could brace themselves, fell, headlong, dragging with him his two friends and skillful guides to death together at the bottom of the ice-filled gorge!

One early evening in July I rode a fascinating mountain path hung with wild scramble of foliage that brushed my face and perfumed my nostrils, into a narrow valley that abruptly came together at the upper end where a wooden hotel squatted right at the foot of great overhanging rocks full of leafy trees and bunches of fern. From here the corkscrew path led in dizzy, vertical spirals, up past the roof of the hotel, and on until it was lost in the clouds—up to the dreaded Pas de la Gemmi, and beyond, to the **Sea-of-Death** Glacier.

Tourists were coming and going. The clatter of Alpine shoes and alpenstock told the eagerness of experienced mountaineers—tourists filling the diligence for down the valley, and others being shown their rooms in the quaint hostelry, in great anticipation of their climb on the morrow to the wildest Pass in the Alps. The smell of mountain pine and laurel, spruce and fir, was in the house. Wild sweetness, on cool currents of air, streamed in at the open windows. From my room I looked down on the descending

WITHOUT A CENT

valley where the mountain brook raved and tore, as if to say: "Ha! Ha! write me down, if you dare, you world tourist. Describe my scampers in these dells, if you can, but leave me to myself, mad with the passion of flinging myself headlong from rock to rock."

Ever been on a vacation? Ever taken to your room in a wonderful part of the world? The porter has set down your luggage, and seen that you have water and towels. As soon as he leaves, you look around, or you throw yourself on the soft bed. Then you go and look out of the window. Then you wash your hands and look out of the window again. Then you sit in the window, and look up and down. You don't intend to jump out during the night, or run away with the bed, but you want to see things, from your window. The waterfall sends up misty spray of vapor that adds to the coolness of the high altitude, and the odor of decaying leaves is pleasant. The big, rough beams in the ceiling, the big rocking-chair, the pictures of fine scenery on the walls, make you smile and feel at home. Others are coming and going. Some of these you have met in another part of the Alps. The hum of animated conversation on the big piazza reaches your ear. Odors of steak and fresh-ground coffee mixing with the delicious tang of nourishing dishes of the Swiss chef, float up to your room and tell you to join other tourists in the Dining Hall.

Early next morning I pushed my wheel up the steepest path to the most frightful Pass in my climbing, where at times it was almost impossible to go on. Up and up, around and around, in and out, now on frail platforms out over the abyss, now on a path cut from the vertical rocks, with railings too trifling for safety, while furzy trees in the valley dropped lower and lower, I crawled, my heart beating fast from the pure glee of climbing. When I reached the gloomy Dauben Lake Inn lying half-upset in a desolate snow-covered sink some miles back from the vertical climb. I was served mutton that rivalled, in wild, gamey flavor, that of Wales. Then I hurried on, for the Pass is broad, the weather fickle. In spots the snow was five feet deep, and the path had not been cleared of the recent storm. A monk, astride a mountain sledge drawn by an old mule, was slowly moving towards me. Soon the mule began to wabble in the deep snow, then floundered flat right in front of me. I worked my way to his side, and lifted him on his crooked, shaky legs, the poor fellow trying to shake the snow from his body, and to wag his stumpy tail at the same time, in gratitude, with a look of shame at his awkardness. Behind him, the fat monk, helpless as a hedge-hog, grinned as he smoked on his excuse for a sled.

At last, ahead of me, right at the very edge of the most fearful looking precipice, with ugly scarred peaks thrusting their bony arms into the clear blue, was the Wildstrubel Hotel, savagely alone, while over it, white and terrible, in celestial shroud of purest snow, gleamed, miles away, the Bernese Oberland in appalling panorama. The hotel sets uneasy on a jag of rock that flies away precipitously for sixteen hundred feet, stopping down there, for want of more material. You shudder a new kind of shudder just to lean over and try to look down, and few tourists can do it. For pure wildness the scene here is probably unsurpassed on all the globe. On one side a half mile of atmosphere; on the other, bleak, snow-checked rocks with pitfalls no trained climber would care to venture over after dark. Back from the hotel, at an acute angle with the Dauben path, was an uncertain path that lost its way towards the Death-Glacier, lying a few miles up. The snow-storm had not reached this rocky barrier, though the frail flowers struggling in the rocks longed for a more hospitable world, doing their utmost to hold up their pitiful bleached stems and faint-scented petals to make the

WITHOUT A CENT

tourist feel less afraid amid the haggard features, as they clustered near each other for protection.

I set out, with camera and alpenstock, for the lower end of the Glacier, soon having to pick my own path along the glacial bed where the erosion of centuries had carved great fissures, and chiselled horrid cavities in the flintlike rock down which poured streams of ice-cold water—a furrowed plain honey-combed with bottomless pits. With daylight and fair skies I could find my way back over these subterranean wells along the distorted backbone of the flattened crest. I had not planned for the blizzard brewing to the west and already gathering over the glacier itself.

I came upon two Germans from Strasburg who joined me. For a mile or so we scrambled over boulders and around sharp-edged cavities, crossing and following a turbulent stream rushing deep down its age-worn channel, to reach a wide, smooth lay of rock where half a dozen little gullies ran over the smooth glacial bed after being churned by the speed and roughness into green-tinted foam. From the main valley we dipped into a smaller one with a good sized stream that lost itself abruptly in the sand, or pouring headlong down the jagged throats of the larger fissures, choked with guttural pain to free itself. Big flakes of snow now fell as we began to scale a cliff leading off toward the terminal moraine of the glacier. Calling out their "Adieu" my companions turned back, hurrying towards the hotel. I pushed forward the more rapidly, hoping to reach if not explore the lowest point of the glacier, which I believed lay just behind another ridge, ignoring the rapid fall of temperature with the rising wind, and hoping to tell my story after supper around the fireplace to astonished tourists from several continents.

To my back I strapped my camera, using both hands to climb the slippery slope of a portion of mountain that possibly none other had tried. Hill after hill, crag after crag arose in my way. No sooner did I scale one wall when another, and another, steeper and higher, confronted me. Strange looking peaks leered on both sides. Unexpected gorges opened. Gushing gullies blocked my way.

At last I reached a foothold on a dizzy shelf where by juking and peering into the blinding snow I caught a glimpse of the ice of the glacier where the big rifts prevented the snow from collecting. Still contending with wall and weather I wormed up a second shelf, clinging long enough to see the backbone of the medial moraine as from beneath this sea of ice a boisterous flood gushed forth and smashed its muddy spray over boulders lying where they fell from the back of the monster. The very danger rivetted me to the scene until my hand slipped, and I dropped back to the lower scarf.

Unable to force a short-cut I tried successively three different ascents, each time finding my hard climbing over the slippery rock had been in vain. Then I sought a way around the ledge by hugging the vertical wall and "toeing" its weathered base to a break in the outcropping where I swung myself above only to find another trap. Darkness was coming prematurely. The snow was blinding. I had no time to lose.

So I let myself down much as I had gone up, hand under hand, until I reached and held to the lower shelf where my feet vainly sought a landing. Dangling in mid-air I lost my hold and dropped—some twenty feet, landing head foremost, rolling and somersaulting into a bank of old snow below which I heard the roar of water. To escape this I held to the side of the wall, pulling off handfuls of rotten shale until I reached an escarpment below me, where by the aid of my alpenstock I swung myself to the other side of the projecting edge.

My tracks had been snowed shut, but as the direction was mostly downwards I hurried along the

SWITZERLAND AND ITALY

Geological Strata

ITALY

stream that now had emerged from the snow, knowing that it emptied somewhere lower in the valley. Time and again I came to the brink of a precipice too steep to try, only to turn back and go over the same dangers again, seeking a way down.

I decided to stay. From stones lying about I built a shelter, cleared out the snow, capped it with the flattest rocks I could find, gathered my coat about me and crawled in, to await daylight and good weather. The wind died down, but the snow fell heavier. Zero weather was coming. The drowsy sensation of sleep fell upon me. But by morning I would be snowed in, with the danger from avalanches covering me, and while I slept I might freeze to death, to say nothing of wild animals. So I gave up my lodge of rocks and set out again for the hotel. Then I came to the second valley which I remembered, picking my way around the glacier wells, stumbling into some of them, and reaching the lower bluff on the other side of which I expected to find the deep-flowing stream which I had crossed by a log high up from the rushing flood. On my hands and knees I crawled, aided by the alpenstock, up the snowy side to the slippery top when to my joy I saw the log not very far to the side, over which I straddled, and after a few more strides saw the faint ray of a light which I followed, to the hotel.

Most of the guests had retired. In the hall were the long rows of shoes awaiting the porter's cleaning, and in the dining-room the landlady, awaiting my coming at this midnight hour to give me a big pair of frowsy slippers in exchange for my wet shoes, and to serve me hot ribble-soup, roast beef, and cherry dessert, as I told of my climb. She was contemplating making up a party of guides with St. Bernards to search the mountains for me.

Two days later I descended by a path-stairway even more dangerous than the one I had ascended on the other side, having to lock one of the wheels so as to act as a brake as I brought the bike down with me.

I was now ready to leave a country where graft was unknown, where public servants were controlled by wholesome checks; where income taxes are graded with regard to surplus sums; where school books, pencils and paper are free; where you may send a barrel of salt or a load of hay by mail; a telegram for six cents, through the post office; ride comfortable trains night and day for a week for less than it costs to go from Chicago to St. Louis; where your baggage is handled carefully and sent ahead, if you desire; where everything is done to benefit all the people—railroads, telegraphs, telephones owned and operated by them.

On the seventeenth of July I climbed the great St. Bernard Pass, looking down as I ascended, upon green meadows in which quiet-eyed kine grazed, and upon hundreds of gleaming little wheat fields that goldened in the evening sun as it flooded the warm valley of the Rhone and hastened the wheat for the sickle. There is no rural beauty comparable to an Alpine sylvan scene when viewed from a lofty eminence in fair weather at sunset. Big St. Bernards came down the mountain side to greet me and to lend assistance if needed, leading me to the guest-door of the Hospice, where a monk received me, assigning me Room No. 21 with the picture of George Washington on the wall. Wine was passed, and as is customary, each guest poured for the other. I turned my glass upside down and declined to put the wine to my brother's lips. One of the guests had refilled his glass several times, imbibing rather freely of the food and drink freely furnished. Filling my glass with cold water I held it up:

"God made this; it is better than your wine."

"Man made this!" he replied, holding his wine aloft.

"No!" I replied, "not man, but le diable!" when the guests laughed at the man sousing himself.

COASTING INTO ITALY

With my feet upon the coaster brake I began to glide into Italy, when, passing through a mass of clouds, two army officers of the Alpine Guard ordered me to halt. Satisfied I was only a tourist they waved me from other armed men hiding in the rocks and allowed me to proceed.

How I did turn curves and bounce and leap! What silvery roads o'erhung with verdant suggestions of sunny Italy! The scenery was of the most wildly romantic, changing from the grand into the awful, dissolving at every turn into astonishing vistas. My only care was to watch the sharp curves and steer across the narrow bridges, and ride, balancing on my steed and filling my swelling chest with samples of a dozen different atmospheres, at first cool and rare, then warm and fragrant, soft with the gentlest touch of sweet-whispering valley-born winds. Below me a thundering stream broke into rapids or churned its greenish flood into spasms of terror as its great force thrashed the gray rocks far below its deep banks!

Though only twenty minutes from Switzerland the scene had changed. No longer did pretty children smile or wave dimpled hands, and none lifted their cap, as they did in Tell's land, the little, hard, dark eyes in contrast to the big blue of the thrifty Swiss. Beggars at the side of the road held out dirty little tins for coppers.

Farms were little, with fences of wood, wire, hedge and stone. Towns were littered with filth, with few lawns, and dirty houses of stone and mortar, while cows bawled about the streets stealing fruit from hucksters' carts, the women gathering their offal with their bare hands, then with basket upon their heads they'd wabble down the street threatening to collide with you and douse you with what was meant for the garden. The shops were small, untidy and unclean. Calico was sold over the same counter with chocolate, and postage stamps with cigars, cookies at the harness shop. The proprietor, usually a woman, sits outside knitting. If you wait long enough she may come in and get what you want, if she has it, which is seldom. At the hotels bread was served me in slender sticks, three feet long, and about as thick as a pencil. Soups were good and also the new dishes fried in butter and flavored with mints.

The Italian lakes nestle like well-bred kittens in the lower lap of the rosey-hued Alps. I boarded the graceful little boat at Arona to enjoy one of the sweetest pleasure-trips of my tour, on Lake Maggiore, the largest, as its name suggests, of the three— Maggiore, Lugano, and Como. While sailing in and out of the sweeping bays, enchanted by an ever-changing pageant of magic tinted water, bluest of skies and fairest of mountains, through some deep gorge of which gleamed in the distance the snow-mantled Alps, I extemporized:

> Maggiore, sweet Italian!
>   Glassy blue and dimpled green,
> Softly straying 'mong the mountains,
>   Come, and be my sunny Queen!
>
> Maggiore, gentle maiden!
>   Love not others far away,
> I am dreaming on thy bosom,
>   In thy charming lap I lay.
>
> Maggiore, sky-loved water!
>   Play not truant with thy grace;
> I will take thee with me ever,
>   I will always see thy face.
>
> Maggiore, sun-kissed Maggie!
>   Break not soon my spell of thee,
> Keep my thoughts with thee, forever.
>   Lover true I'll ever be.

WITHOUT A CENT

And while lying in the lap of this pretty Italian girl—I mean lake, I read from a newspaper in Italian: "Le Pape Morte!" (The Pope is dead.) The public funeral was to be held in St. Peters at Rome. So, at the very next landing I said farewell to the Captain, whose guest I was, and left the boat.

At sunset I reached the picturesque beach of Como where the glorious charm of calm beauty spread her poised wing as I stood in rapture. Before me a giant opal, set in amethyst, sapphire and emerald. Each wooing breeze that kissed her dimpled cheek lay where it touched, forgetful of its mission from yonder cloud-wreathed purple peak, drowned by its own ecstasy in the mirrored resplendence of a thousand hues.

I reached Milan at midnight where I rested on a bench until dawn, by the Cathedral. The longer I looked the greater and whiter it grew. Tremendous is its size, bewildering are its intricate embellishments. The daring originality of its flying buttresses compels the attention of architect and tourist alike. Beaten by thousands of storms, eroded at the joints by weathering, its graceful sweep in curve preserves intact the harmony that was first in the mind of the builder, the foundation of which was begun one hundred and six years before Columbus sailed. It is a cathedral with ninety-eight pinnacles and two thousand spires, each crowned by heroic sized statues keeping their silent vigil over the city throughout the centuries. As the first rays of the sun kissed with gold the needle peaks of this mountain of marble it was more like a dream than a reality.

The air was balmy at Genoa, and I threw myself upon one of the iron benches in a little park where there was a statue of Columbus, when another bum—I mean another man, pretended to be asleep on another bench opposite me, but who watching me closely meant to rob me when I fell asleep. So I stood up, with Columbus—my friend globe-trotter—

AROUND THE WORLD

lighted my lamp and rode about this tropical city. Loads of swells were coming home from soirees. Some were dressed, and some were undressed—I mean some were in their evening dress. At a shop a baker was mixing his dough in a vat in the window. Barefoot, he rolled high his trousers, jumped in upon it, then seizing an overhead strap with both hands he held on while pummeling the dough with his feet, working his toes back and forth to remove the surplus. At dawn I rode the Riviera along the Mediterranean, with breakfast at a fashionable resort where I hoped they baked their own bread. The air was scented with vanilla, the water from wells tasted of it, and soon my clothes and kerchief were flavored with it— as I rode through vanilla orchards.

Suddenly, ahead of me some miles, I saw a big tower in the act of falling, but to my surprise it did not go down, but just hung there, half over. Then I recalled the Leaning Tower of Pisa and I was in that very neighborhood! When I walked under it I hurried through, for it surely did look as if it meant to come on down. Then I went into the historic church where the swinging of the bronze lamp suggested to Galileo our modern pendulum.

In Rome

The doors of St. Peter's were to close at eleven o'clock, so I pumped up my tires and rode to look for a lodging, get my breakfast and then ride to the Funeral in time to see the Pope. On the other side of a wonderful fountain arose from the most commanding position in the City a stately structure, set with great marble pillars, on the roof of which I read: GRAND HOTEL. This fashionable hotel had not been recommended to me, but I felt it was safe. So I rode through the park of palms and flowers frequented by the guests, deciding to come here myself after I had registered and breakfasted. Twice my wheel fell down where I leaned it against a thirty-foot marble pillar, making so much noise I needed no further announcement of my arrival. I was there. Everybody knew it. My wheel put on no "airs," and acted the same as it did when it stood in Mrs. Moriarity's hen-yard. But both of us more than half expected to be chased out before we got in.

Instantly when I had told my mission, my name went down on the register. "Breakfast is ready," said the manager, as distinguished tourists gathered around the wheel. "Make this your home while in Rome."

No millionaire ever so rich. It meant recognition of the worth of my adventure, confirmed my own confidence in it, and steadied my growing enthusiasm. In the grandest dining-hall in all Europe I ordered my full table d'hote breakfast at nine, eating peaches, pears and figs before the lamb-chops, eggs and coffee with toast, feasting my eyes upon the art-gallery walls and ceiling in gold, and thinking of the poor bum back at Genoa.

Then I rode to the Cathedral, miles away, past the Forum and its acres of falling pillars, then over the Tiber, as Caesar before me had swam it.

At a little before the closing of the doors I pushed aside the heavy leathern curtain of the great doorway, the portal of which was set with columns forty-eight feet high, surmounted by a parapet supporting two hundred and thirty-two statues, taking my first excited glimpse of the greatest cathedral in the world, and saw the mortal remains of a Pope.

I descended into the prison where Peter and Paul were held, and saw the catacombs for miles underground. After five days of seeing Rome to the full from my wheel, I rode out on the old Roman road for Florence, knowing that I was to return and see the coronation of a new Pope. That night I slept in a wheat field with two sheaves for a pillow and four for a cover, in the dreaded Campagna fever-fens! The next night I lodged in the home of a poor family, with chicory for coffee.

The third day I was in the wild Apennines, steep and rough, one mountain right after another, where the soil and contour were volcanic.

On a sharp curve I had a hard fall down the mountain side, tearing my clothing badly, bruising and scratching my body, and breaking off a pedal, forty miles from town. In this condition I was refused food at the huts of these hill folk, not so much because they had none as because they thought it was not good enough. In one of these hovels the man sneaked into the kitchen and pushed his frail wife in to meet me. He did not know that his wretched hospitality would have been as welcome to me as the luxuriance of the Grand. That night a farmer turned me away from his haybarn, fearing I might smoke and burn him out. Then I crawled into the top of a wheat-stack, pulling out a few of the sheaves to get a hold and keep from falling out of bed during the night. There is nothing like sleeping in an Italian strawstack with the heavens for your ceiling and the grand pageantry of innocent memories crowding the galleries of your fertile mind. Every artist hopes to see Florence. Ruskin wrote of it. George Eliot's Romola describes it. Here is where Michael Angelo and Andrea del Sarto were turned loose upon new creations in color and form. The eye tires at the many gems of the renaissance, where both Ufficzi and Pitti Palaces are filled with thousands upon thousands of masterpieces. Here is but one: Cain, in bronze, stands in a sylvan scene. With his right hand he thrusts from his sight the murder that now stings his memory; lashed by conscience he is goaded to frenzy. His left hand spurns the vision of spring and life, and to the lovely maiden, tripping with fairy feet over the green meadow, garlands in her delicate hands, and wreath to crown, he turns his back. Amid this tranquil beauty, flooded with sunshine and happiness of playing children, Cain

WITHOUT A CENT

wanders through his own Hell of hideous shapes and sounds.

After standing at the spot where Savonarola was burned I took the road again, resting my face that had been twisted out of shape in admiring wonder of miles and miles of art. The sun was dazzling hot. The air was sizzling dry. But the shade was all the cooler, and the fountains gushed the coldest water.

In a valley was a cattle-fair where hundreds of white oxen were shown. I caught a pair of these on the road, both snowy white, horns exactly alike, heads the same, ears flopping alike, eyes of same color and size, keeping step with each other—

"Two minds with but a single thought,
Two hearts that beat as one."

Farmers were thrashing wheat in four different ways: by tramping it out with animals; by beating the sheaf over a stump or rock; by a flail, and by a steam-thresher.

The young men in towns to whom I showed my letter of introduction in Italian could seldom read their own language, these street loafers or lower class youths were so illiterate.

On the second morning I passed the XLVII mile stone out of Rome, and then, rounding a curve on the hill, the VII one, when the splendid view of the City of Seven Hills, seen often from the same spot by Julius Caesar, as he rode on his two-wheeled vehicle, burst into sight.

Once more in Rome I took my meals at the Grand. Chaperoned by their father, I joined two Italian girls in their carriage, to see with them the great event that fairly rocked the city with excitement— the Coronation of a new Pope! We were at St. Peters early. The multitude soon became a surging mob, when children were torn from their parents and never seen again. Women became hysterical and fought their way out with hat-pins. The doors had not yet opened, but as we had pushed up towards the front, we were

AROUND THE WORLD

sure to get in, and so we were very happy. Ahead of us deep rows of soldiers with bayonets fixed and rifles drawn cried to the people to halt. There were too many hundred thousand in that mass to heed such command. So these soldiers tried to push us all back, using their rifles, as I held to the girls to keep them from being thrown and trampled to death. With a mad surge forward at the opening of the doors, the human mass poured in so fast that tickets were not collected. Many had walked for days to see this Coronation. Others had slept in the streets so as to be sure to be in time, and to save the high price asked for rooms, if indeed a single room in Rome was vacant. Thousands had come days before and had booked at the hotels now overflowing into the hallways. Other thousands had reached the city only that morning. Still other thousands were coming. Boats and trains all emptied humanity that poured toward St. Peters. Rome, to her last citizen, was there. American cardinals jostled Italian farmers. The rich and cultured vied with the poor and unlettered—all glad, and mad, to get in!

When hundreds of thousands had filled the inside space, the doors were shut. Outside, with tickets in their hands, thousands begged piteously for admission, grieving over the lost opportunity of a lifetime. Some had crossed the ocean on fast steamers just for the Coronation. But none could get in. THE DOORS WERE SHUT!

Mass and music went on from nine to one. It was a most joyful crowd. There was but one language, that of the heart, and the face was its tongue. Thousands of nuns in black and white, thousands of monks in black and brown, bowed low as the priest was borne in on the Pontifical Chair, and the Triple Crown about to be set upon his head. By me was a little old woman of about eighty-five, in faded calico. She had evidently slept in the street as I had slept at the Grand. But she was so little she was not going to see the Coronation after all. So, when the Crown was held aloft, I offered to lift her, and by her smile I knew I might. My own mother was at that very moment hovering near death in a Catholic Hospital. In my next letter which I was to get at Jerusalem, I was to know whether she rallied, or died!

After being a millionaire for nine days I said good-bye to the manager, received my wheel from the "Bell-boys," and by the sun saw that it was about two o'clock. I rode out of the city by the Appian Gate, as Paul had walked in before me, he to be beheaded, and I to go on around the world!

Off for Vesuvius

From Rome to Naples is an ever-changing picture of hill, valley, mountain and sea. Apples, pears and figs could be picked from the roadside where quaint shacks of straw held human beings, where the Ford was a little donkey, the farmers too poor to afford the real auto. Thieving among them seemed to be common. Returning from town a farmer discovered that his neighbor had carried off a dozen of his wheat shocks during his absence, setting them up in his own field. So he picked out his own grain and set them all back again, adding a few of his neighbor's shocks for good measure!

On a road that seemed to have no turning I rode all night, slowly and without a light, for many tramps lay sleeping at right angles to the road, their feet almost to the edge of the wagon track, and I rode my wheel on her "tip-toes," with muscles set, nerves alert, ready to dash forward at full speed if one of them should try to stop me. At a country cottage sometime after midnight a lover was serenading his sweetheart. The moon hung low. Dark shadows flung athwart the yard. The air was still and warm. Right below her window played the swain on a guitar, and when I slowed up to watch the sight, she came to the window in her nightie! I longed for a sweetheart myself, but without contesting his claims I speeded up again, the soft, sweet music of the romantic hour fading in the distance.

Naples was the climax of beggars, noise and dirt. From my hotel on the sea I rode for Vesuvius, the streets growing narrow in that part of the city where macaroni is made. Squeezed through little pipes this delicious food is then hung out on the line to dry, like clothes, where dust from passing vehicles settles upon it and the flies roost, making it the best macaroni in the world! I always ask for "spaghetti" made in Naples. It is the best.

The same volcano that had buried Pompeii two thousand years before was now again soon to send thousands to their death. The government forbade the ascent of tourists. "The government" being absent I began my bicycle ride up the old furnace, as it smoked furiously and now and again hurled great belches of lava high in the air. I would have made better headway if an officer on horseback had not bothered me so much. He said I would be arrested, and for positive rudeness to have his own way I never saw his equal. A couple of times he rode his horse over me, but did not damage my wheel very much. I pushed him and his horse down off the path oftener than he pushed me and my wheel off. Trying thus to push each other off, his horse soon was winded. Then he dismounted and tried to stop me from the ground, but I didn't wait. At the half-way hut I abandoned my wheel, but finding the price of water too high for my pocket, plodded on in the dry tufa that dusted my fevered lips and let me sink knee deep in its baking heat. Reaching a private road leading to a stone wall and a gate, I sat down by the post, covering my head from the fierce rays of the awful sun, hoping somehow the locked gate would be opened for me, when a man came out of the little house and ordered me to go back. Then his daughter came to draw water from a cistern, saying:

WITHOUT A CENT

"Papa, let him in!"

The gate flew open, as I rushed to the cistern to help the girl draw the water, filling myself and bottle at the same time, without which I could not have made the ascent. Ten winding spirals led me to the top, past the stream of lava five feet deep as it broke over the path, hissing and sputtering and wriggling like an angry serpent from Hell. Fumes of sulphur and hydrochloric acid rising in clouds of dust under my feet irritated my eyes and nose and almost suffocated me, while the heat rapidly increased as I ascended. Hundreds of fissures opened all around me from which issued hissing steam and smoke. The ground shook in convulsions. My shoes were smoking. My clothing was scorching. Some guides who lost their lives when the top blew off, were still risking the danger zone, looking after any parties who might make the ascent for scientific purposes. After a longer pause than usual the mountain began to tremble as if in mortal agony when the lava shot straight into the sky in wrathful defiance of heaven's law that chained its terrific energy in the narrow vault of the mountain. Hurled high in the air, big stones dropped at my feet. My guide pulled me with him as we fled down the volcano's side. This was the volcano that blew her brains out on that side of the Globe, and kicked over San Francisco on this side!

TWO WEEKS ON THE MEDITERRANEAN

In a row-boat my wheel and I are taken out to the ship lying at anchor. The music made by my hand running through the limpid water sings to my listening ear and throbbing heart. More of us are poets than editors and neighbors recognize. Our trouble is in telling it. The delirium of joy robs the power to crystallize the rapture into ordinary words. As a test of your own poetry, rock with me on the blue Bay of Naples as the city recedes, fading into purplish mystery, old Vesuvius gushing liquid fire from her recent wounds, and rising out clearer as we glide on this Sea of the Carthaginians! Yonder the rocks stand hundreds of feet from the water. There, Magic Capri, whose grottoed rainbows play with blue sky and crimson sunset. But best of all, there's my ship, for my ship has come in! Not a big liner, but with graceful bow and gentle swell, big enough and high enough out of the water to be safe and homey.

The boatman takes his twenty centimes, looks up at the Captain, and rows back, when I present my ticket that calls for meals and a "place on deck." I am on a traveling hotel for two weeks, and my board is paid! Two weeks of just going, with rest for my legs and work for my mind, sleeping safe from wild cattle and fierce banditti. The whistle sounds. The boat churns the sea and swings around. From below, in little boats, rises music from musicians. But the sweetest music is heard only by the "inner ear."

The next day we steamed into the classy Bay of Palermo, capital and chief city of the Island of Sicily. The "Letimbro" lay here till night, giving me ample time to see the city, where little donkeys laden with fruit and kids stumbled over frisking dogs. Less than a third as big as Ireland, and one-tenth as big as Kansas, the weight of the mighty past oppresses the student of this little world. Over this rocky isle are strewn the heroic myths of Ulysses and Vulcan. Descendants of many races jostled me in the streets, the pure Greek face with oval form admired by Titian, with black, lustrous eyes and low forehead, full cheek, pug nose and little mouth; the Spaniard, with proud setting down of heel; negroes with black, curly hair, thick lips and tawny skin. Along the streets grew the pepper tree, while the esplanades blazed forth with gorgeous Judas trees and elephant-leaf.

All night we sailed on a sea of glass, passing through the narrow channel between Italy and Sicily where Scylla and Charybdis ruled.

I slept on deck on a bed of canvas, awaking, just

ITALY AND SICILY

Sicilian Kiddies Greeting the Author

TURKEY

This Launch Rescued the Author

WITHOUT A CENT

as the sun in crimson glow poured its glory over the sea, the "Letimbro" slowing up for Catania and making fast to a huge stone wall built out into the Bay. With a day and a half ashore and a home at the best hotel that looked right down into the busiest street, I "lived and moved," buying transparent seedless grapes that melted in my mouth like perfumed dew, and delicious ripe figs, sixteen for a cent, from hawkers riding braying donkeys—to say nothing of pears, peaches, plums and prunes, all of the best tasting I ever ate. Youngsters followed me, curious to see the cyclist who was riding around the world. One of these kiddies had rushed out in his nightgown— he reminded me of the boy Jesus—and I took his picture and gave him a hug. The bare hills back of the city caused me to ask the reason. "Diboscamento," said one, which means deforesting. The Sicilian forests had been wantonly destroyed by ruthless dollar-chasers, and not replaced. Her private capitalists had robbed her of her greatest asset, for as soon as the trees had gone, the rains went. "Diboscamento" means no lakes, no brooks, no spring, no fruit, or flowers, or wheat, or corn. It means cold winters and hot summers. England, the most abundant in trees, is the most salubrious. "Diboscamento" is the present curse of the United States, for our representatives at Washington, by bribe or otherwise, allow private corporations to rob us of our fine forests without so much as making them replant as many trees as they cut down, robbing the land of its noblest and most necessary asset, making travel in those regions like a hideous nightmare. We should not only plant more trees than we destroy, but we should also plant, on both sides of the road running north and south, and on the south side of the road running east and west, fruit, nut, lumber and ornamental trees, thus increasing the scenic beauty of our landscape, make rural drives more pleasant, the climate more equable, and adding untold wealth to the nation.

Sicily is today bleak and bare. What she raises from the ground must be done by irrigation.

Crete rises high in bleak mountains with vineyards hiding in the valleys, the blue sea kissing its scarred edges and cooling the heat of a tropical sun. Hucksters in boats hurried to us with white and purple grapes, and big bursting figs, black and blue. In getting my change from the boy I got some small coins in five and ten leptas so that when we reached Athens on the morrow I could hire a boatman to take me ashore and be able to pay him in his own coin.

"Graeca!" cried a sailor running to me from the ship's kitchen, pointing to the rising shore line. Higher and higher the little country of Demosthenes rose out of the sea until the mountains back of Athens stood out keen and clear in the rarest of rare atmospheres. I dropped into the first rowboat and was the first to land, and as the train for Athens, six miles away, was just now due to leave, I ran for the depot. The gate-keeper saw me coming, had a ticket ready, and punched it, as I caught the last coach. At Athens I asked the first Athenian I met the way to the Acropolis.

"Akropolis!" he said, pointing to the right. We both spoke Greek!

I hit the path on a hard run, glad for the outdoor exercise on land, and was climbing, and then on top of Mars Hill in less than a minute, stumbling over platforms, pillars, images and statues—a gloriously ghastly wreck. "And this is the Parthenon!" I exclaimed to myself, my heart beating like a drum as I walked beneath the marble wreckage of ages. From temple to temple I sprinted, studying rapidly elaborate frieze and cornice, sitting in the old marble seats of the theatres, the names of those long-gone playgoers still carved upon them. As some of the ruins were so much more worn than others I sought the cause: The Romans who conquered the Greeks, built here some of their temples, but their work, even

WITHOUT A CENT

though much later, was not so well preserved as that of the Greeks. The same storms chilled them. The same volcanoes shook them. There was one difference: honest workmanship of the Greeks. It was noon when I walked through the theatre of Dionysius seating three thousand, where ages ago the plays of Sophocles and Euripides were heard. The players had made their final exits. The rich and cultured patron had gone—and all because of what Paul brought to Athens—the certain definite God whose greater wisdom and splendor made those marble cuttings look like pig-pens!

I was about to make my descent into Athens when two girls in bright colors came up Mars Hill, the daughters of the Captain and Mate, on vacation from a Genoa college, when I ran to them and helped them up the steep grade from Mars Hill to the Acropolis, then down to lunch at Hotel Pateros.

Back on the Acropolis again, I looked off into the Plain of Marathon, where Darius was defeated by Miltiades, and then at the Plain of Attica, a little farther back, the atmosphere clearer than that of Colorado or Switzerland. I was studying again the innumerable fragments of history in broken and fallen marbles, when looking toward the sea I was startled to see smoke from the the funnel of the "Letimbro" rise in big, black clouds, firing up for her sail to Turkey. I caught the train bearing the two girls to the beach and then in a row-boat to their fathers' ship, where on the clean deck I stretched my legs as I gazed upon the passing grandeur of Acropolis and mountain background, the sun pouring down upon her treasure-fields the golden splendor of Summer's sunshine. I saw the same scene as it was twenty-three centuries before the "Letimbro" throbbed with steam-filled cylinders below me. The Parthenon gleamed strangely near. Yonder Corinthian pillar and Doric shaft, columns of ineffaceable beauty, looked down upon Homer as he walked in

AROUND THE WORLD

ecstatic meditation. Along the frieze of the Olympian temple of Jove, Phidias crawled with chisel and hammer, giving last touches to his imperishable masterpiece. There on that Hill the world's greatest poetry, oratory, and architecture first spread wings of flight to other continents.

Little islands rose grandly around us as we changed our course, now for one and now for another of these amethysts of the Aegean. The long rays of the setting sun tipped with silvered gold the receding columns on the Hill. Night stole softly over land and sea, when moonlight hung the sinking shoreline with gauzy dreams.

Up to date, August 27. I had ridden 13,650 miles, crossing fifteen countries, with 26,350 miles yet to go.

IN TURKEY MY TROUBLES BEGIN

Scores of funny long row-boats with sharp prows hurried out to us in the bay at Smyrna, each boatman calling loudly for his share of passengers and baggage—mine following me down the street and demanding a second fee. It was Sunday and business was in full swing. It was like a great circus just to be on the streets. Donkeys and camels did most of the carrying, walking right on the sidewalks, like a train of cars. Seven camels were usually tied together, and these to a donkey, which led them, each about fifteen feet apart, while three bells, one within the other, were placed on the last camel to warn people at the head of the donkey, one hundred and twenty-five feet away, to look out!

At the College I was engaged to give lessons in physical culture. The Christians were having a hard time in competing with the Turks who boycotted them and otherwise injured their business and comfort. It seemed so strange to worship in a Christian church here in one of the cities of the "Seven Churches," and to sing the world-loved hymn, "Nearer, My God, to Thee," in Greek—"Egguteron, Pros Ton, Theon."

Wishing to go to Ephesus by rail, one of the

WITHOUT A CENT

Armenian students was sent to show me the way to the depot. Somewhere on the route he turned aside and led me up to a sweet-shop where I bought him a generous package of candy. Then he led me into that part of town where the greatest numbers of "eats" and "drinks" were to be had. For two hours he kept me going, halting right in front of a lemonade stand or candy stall, piloting me so fast as to require the greatest quantity of refreshment in that hot and dusty town. We first had a red glass of something, then a yellow glass, then a clear one, meanwhile eating our way through the whole list of Ottoman sweets until I had set up everything in sight to this young scamp. The sweat from frequent imbibing of temperance drinks poured over my clean collar, while the terrible dust from the dirty streets settled into my clothes with grimy vengeance.

"Why don't we get there?" I asked impatient.

"I don't know," he replied.

Brigands were infesting the suburbs of Smyrna. Tourists had been warned of them and asked to remain at home. A big price was on the head of the leader, Tchakigis, for he warred against the Turks rather than foreigners. His policy was to capture a rich man or woman, or some one for whom he believed a big ransom would be paid. Once in his hands there was no escape if the money was not forthcoming, his severity being due to the act of treachery inflicted upon his father, also a brigand, who on being promised his freedom if he would lay down his weapons in the city square, was immediately executed. The infuriated son determined to exact the last farthing for this Turkish perfidy. As his quarrel lay with the Turks, the natural foe of Christians, I had little fear of him, and with a Greek guide rode into the hills, carrying our wheels where we could not ride, and stopping long enough at a fig tree to eat what we wanted and fill our pockets with this fine food, reasoning that if we should accidentally come upon this outlaw, this extra food would come in handy. This tree, as was most fig trees, was about fifteen feet high, well-branched, and evidently bearing more fruit than would pay its taxes—for trees in Turkey were taxed, whether they bore fruitage, or not, and because of this abominable law, many trees which might bear fruit if given a chance, were cut down by the owner, thus robbing the land of one of its chief assets. Like most fig trees, the fruit on this one could not be seen, its deeply-scalloped leaf hiding it. The Saviour once turned aside to such a fig tree to examine closely, as I did here, for fruit—he finding nothing but leaves.

We came upon a rude mountain tavern where one of the two wild men we met gave us a scare—we thought he must be Tchakigis! We were not so much mistaken, for the bandit had been there just before us, where he hurriedly gulped down some coffee, grabbed up a package of cigarettes, leaped to his horse and was off. Like him, we took our coffee in gulps.

With a missionary I went by rail to Ephesus, forty-one miles away, the only refreshing scene that of white grapes strewn in great patches on the ground to cure. Shrivelled by the hot sun and dry air, the peasants shovelled them into big heaps when they were put into big baskets and bags. It did seem so queer to ride into E-p-h-e-s-u-s! the city to which Paul wrote his letter to the Ephesians. All about us were fields of fallen pillars, crushed pedestals, and broken statues, victims on the deserted battlefield of defeated gods. Right out of the ruins of the Temple of Diana grew a fig tree full of most excellent figs, many of them curing right on the tree. I climbed up and picked all we wanted, and not a rascal priest of that Diana faith was there to keep me down.

Back at the station we were eating a watermelon when a peasant woman and her daughter tried to buy their tickets for less than the regular fare, for orientals "dicker" with sellers by "haggling." These

WITHOUT A CENT

women, unused to railroads, were so ignorant they thought they could "reduce the fare."

"Too much," said the mother, in Turkish, and moved away as if about to set out afoot. The ticket agent was calm. Then she came back and laid down some coins.

"Must have more," said the agent.

"We can't go, mother," said the girl, "that's all we have."

The third time she laid down money. The third time it was pushed back. After much fumbling under outlandish garments, the daughter finally fished up another coin, showing no evident surprise at finding it.

"Now, that's all!" said the mother vehemently.

The train pulled in, as the agent turned to other duties. The passengers went aboard. The train was ready to leave. Then the mother began a most searching examination of her costume, seen and unseen, finding somewhere in a skirt or other under-garment, another coin, which she laid down, with the rest, crying:

"That's our train. We can't go."

The bell was now ringing for the departure of the train. Then the two worked together in earnest, for the engineer was opening the throttle.

"Get it, Salina!" cried the woman. "We'll get left!"

Then the daughter went down under her clothes once more and, without any hesitation, got the required coin. The ticket was issued, and the two females whose government was barbarously murdering Christians because of their superiority, climbed into the dumpy coach as it began to move into the desert.

No missionary there dare tell half of the truth in a letter home. She may only hint at the frightful plottings to exterminate the Armenians. Until the great nations of the world bring Turkey before them

AROUND THE WORLD

and give her the punishment due her, at once and forever putting a stop to her million massacres, I for one will think they are just fooling us about the League of Nations. Compared to what they did to others, my torture was kind treatment. But I think my own mother would not have known me when I escaped from their hands and was received aboard one of our battleships.

The pitiful cries of a kitten coming from the cellar of a Mohammedan house in Smyrna, where it had fallen through a broken window, made me pause until an unveiled woman happened along when she helped me knock at the door which a young woman opened, as she threw over her face a fuzzy mantle. The woman told her about the kitten and that I wanted to get it, when she stood back to make room for me. By the laws and customs of the land I should not have been admitted, but I was in the house, and at her invitation. Over rich rugs and past divans built into the wall I passed into another room bordered on both sides with silk-hung couches. The girl pointed to a low door into the cellar as she hastened to hide behind a heavy portierre. I hurried, for the one thing I feared was the returning Moslem husband, who finding me in his house would want to kill me on the spot. In the dark and dingy basement I found the kitty as it staggered toward me, nearly dead from exhaustion. With it held securely to my throat I was climbing the dark stairs when heavy footsteps on the back piazza told me of the presence of a man. Nearly falling over a foot-stool in one room, and becoming tangled in the curtains as I hastened into the other, I got out again on the street, the Moslem female having vanished. The man proved to be a eunuch delivering some groceries, but I lost no time in leaving. As the kitten would have been trampled to death by passing camels, I took it with me to the college. Here I washed its face and gave it a saucer of goat's milk which its little pink tongue

WITHOUT A CENT

could not lap up fast enough, its bushy tail sticking straight up, and curling at the end in a sincere "Thank you!" Immediately afterward it fell asleep in my lap. In a suitable wooden box I kept it in my room, bringing it such food as it required.

In the Lawson Packing-House I was told to help myself to a heap of ten tons of figs, and when the women sorting them knew I had ridden my wheel all the way from Polo, and across the ocean, they tossed me the finest ones they could find as they walked around on them with bare feet. Sorted into four grades, these figs were carried to the floor above, where Turks, Armenians, Greeks and Syrians packed them, taking the figs, one at a time, into their two hands, between the thumb and forefinger, splitting the skin on the under side and drawing the fig apart from below, as it was being flattened, then dipping it hurriedly into a pail of sea-water, it was pressed into the box, row after row, and layer after layer. Thus broken and pulled apart on one side, the figs so packed have the appearance of being much larger than they really are, and they pack better and blend more in taste with the other figs. The salt water tends to preserve them, as well as improve the taste, and it prevents the hands of the men becoming "sticky." Smyrna figs lead the world. The sunshine and climate, together with the sting of a certain wasp, make them the superior of all others. This same wasp has been caught in Turkey and imported to California, where it has been bred in great numbers. Figs so "stung" there are called "Calimyrna" figs, and they are much better in taste than other California figs not so stung, looking and tasting much like the real Smyrna fig. So much for being "stung."

Arrested at Constantinople

Engaging a student to feed the kitten in my absence, and giving him a coin with the promise of more coins on my return, I sailed on the "Albania," for a side trip to the Bosphorus. Indented by little bays, and resembling a river rather than a sea, the Aegean was like glass all the way. The atmosphere was veiled by sunlit purple flung with mysterious enchantment that quieted the nerves and inspired my pen:

> The glory of the past is thine,
>   Thou blue Aegean Sea!
> Still rise the Isles enchanted here
>   Like monarchs bold and free.
>
> Thy breath is like a fragrant balm,
>   Thy wavelets soft or wild;
> Thou hast the beauty of the dawn,
>   The passion of a child.

I slept on deck by two Moslems, one of whom forcibly stole my bed space by pushing me aside. As he was a Moslem and I a Christian, and as he carried a dagger, and I an olive-branch, I let him kneel and pray on his rug laid down on my space, while I prayed to my God, on another. We rubbed against each other as we slept, and when I awoke during the night, as I often did, in nervous expectation of something that might happen, I felt of myself to be sure that I was alive, for one of his teachings told him he might have thirty beautiful wives in Heaven for every Christian he would kill here. The Greek sailors disliked these Mohammedans, and took sides with me, as did all the Europeans aboard.

On Sunday morning we ran into the Golden Horn where the Sweet Waters of Europe meet the salty sea, steaming among a lot of Turkish battleships. I looked as meek as I could so they wouldn't fire on us. Some Turks came aboard from a launch, looking furtively among the passengers, one of them at me. I didn't flinch, but his look made me uneasy. Every "bell" on board our ship of life tolls the death of a passing experience, and announces the birth of a new

TURKEY

HOLY LAND

WITHOUT A CENT

force in our career. Before he took his eyes off of me I knew I was a "marked" man.

The sun was rising out of the Black Sea as the "Albania" slowly made her way toward the City of Constantinople, rounding a quadrant of beauty on her seven hills like a Queen of May awakening with the sun, to etch in delicate tracery of silver the bold front of palace and minaret, and fringing with lace-work the cloud-effect half hiding the higher part of the city from us. It was a most brilliant panorama. We had come at the right moment. The big, round sun, so yellow in contrast to the rocky hills of grove and parterre, came up in the right spot for effect, burnishing every point with morning glow. Like the virgin face of the expectant Turkish bride uncovering at the approach of her lover, the storm clouds hanging over the city, foretelling its impending doom, lifted.

All on board felt the grandeur of the scene. The night had been cool. The morning was moist and fragrant. Ozone of electric energy gave snap to the nerves and lustred every eye. Every one seemed fastened to the deck where they stood, in rapt admiration at the unrolling splendor as the City of Constantine, with a mottled history of romance that reads like a nightmare, lay before us.

The "Albania" did not dock at once, but steamed slowly from the shore, affording us a series of ever-changing pictures of the city rising solidly from the water like an elaborate bird-house of giantland. When the anchor finally dropped, I had counted fifty-six minarets, rising straight and defiant above all else, in some of which the muezzin was calling the hour of prayer. A little launch flying the Stars and Stripes drew near. It was the most beautiful of all the sights, and it seemed to say: "Glad you're here. I'll take care of you!"

From hundreds of ships in the harbor waved flags of all nations, the Star and Crescent on many of them.

The only flag that was cheered, was my flag. It was the world's choice—and mine!

"You can't get in on that," said the Customs official, as he handed back my Passport and tried to keep my pocket-knife on the plea that it was a weapon.

"Look here," I said, "this is my Passport. It takes me everywhere!" With shrug of shoulder and slur on lip he was turning away when I opened it and read the description of myself to him.

1st, my age, but I am still unmarried.

2nd, my height—five feet ten inches.

3rd, my forehead—medium; eyes, brown; nose, big; chin, prominent; hair, wavy and black; face, long and thin.

"We can't admit you on that!" he said, more arrogantly.

"But see!" said I, as I pointed to the heading of the Passport:

UNITED STATES OF AMERICA, DEPARTMENT OF STATE.

TO ALL TO WHOM THESE PRESENTS SHALL COME GREETING:

The undersigned, Secretary of the United States of America, hereby requests all to whom it may concern to permit HENRY M. SPICKLER, A CITIZEN OF THE UNITED STATES, SAFELY AND FREELY TO PASS, AND IN CASE OF NEED TO GIVE HIM ALL LAWFUL AID AND PROTECTION.

Honored everywhere, the "Sick Man of Europe" turned it down. Other passengers were examined and checked out, while I was told to stand aside with some low-grade fellows, the passengers looking askance at us as if we were criminals. Guarded by two "Cops," who paced the floor before us like mock generals, we looked it. Then a burly officer in baggy trousers motioned us to follow him. I dropped in behind the others, an officer at my heels.

A halt was made at the entrance to a barracks which we were made to enter. I hesitated, trying to tell them

WITHOUT A CENT

how necessary it was that I meet my friends, though just where I might have found any one I could call a friend in Constantinople I did not know.

Eight o'clock came. Nine, ten, eleven! Sitting around on bundles of clothing, smoking cigarettes or Turkish pipes, my "pardners" passed the time dejectedly. Then I made a test of the situation to see if I were really under arrest. I walked back and forth, then to the door, then out of the door and right back, then whistled "Yankee Doodle." I started again boldly for the door, was outside all right, and planning what street I would take when a guard commanded me to return!

Shortly we were marched through crooked streets solid with houses and shops, two women having been added to our bunch. I wondered if they were to be imprisoned with us. The first "suspect" ahead of me was evidently a Turkish Moor, with head wrapped in black and white cloth. He had the Turk's thick lips and solid chin. His eyes were deep-set, dreamy and black, with a look of deep study. But for the lowly life he had been compelled to live at hard labor his tall straight body would have allowed him to pass for a gentleman of culture. But for his prominent jaws and haggard expression I would have selected him as my room-mate. Next ahead was a young fellow about twenty-five, with curled black mustache, his right leg two inches shorter than his left, bending under heavy luggage in a blanket. He wore the regulation fez and was evidently a Moslem. I would not choose him. The third and fourth were ordinary types met on deck passage on the Mediterranean. Poor, they lived the life of simplest toil, with no ideas of their own and none borrowed.

I was half mad at these simpletons when they turned without protest into a dark court through a big iron gate. Of course I had to follow. Somewhere along here the women dropped out. I made no inquiries but kept on. I soon was alone in a big hall.

Summoned before a magistrate into another room, I was trembling a little as to the motive when a strange coincidence suddenly nerved me into self-possession.

A little maltese kitten with pink mouth, waving its furry tail, and welcoming me by a friendly "meow," suddenly appeared there on the floor, approaching me from the desk. In size, color and action it was the exact copy of the one I had befriended back in Smyrna.

"Kittie!" I called, as it ran toward me looking into my eyes as if it had always known me. With it pressed close to my chin I walked straight to the desk of the now smiling Mohammedan Judge who marvelled that the kittie knew English and had given me its confidence so quickly.

"Are you an American?" he asked.

I pressed my little friend the closer, drew myself up to my full Yankee height, my eye on his, and replied:

"Yes, sir, I am!"

For a brief moment I held his gaze, a moment that was dramatic. That moment seemed to change his mind somewhat. Then he gave orders to an attendant, and I followed him out. My Passport was then taken from me, when I appealed to the United States Consul.

"I wish you would send for him at once," I said; and a page was sent out.

In a short time two heavily armed Moslems returned with the page, big revolvers in their belts, with long swords dangling at their side. They came right up to me and said they were from the United States Consulate and as the Consul was not in, they had come for me. They informed me that I was under arrest because I had come into the city without a Turkish passport. I can not tell how good I felt. My suffering was paid for in the unbounded joy of deliverance by my country. Just to look at the American magazines and newspapers lying on the table here made me feel as if I were right at home among the best of

WITHOUT A CENT

friends. I was to return Monday to see the Consul. In the meantime I could go about the city.

Near the Consulate I came upon the luxurious entrance to the Bristol Hotel, where the manager met me with extended hand, my home for ten days! On Monday I learned that the special passport required was an Imperial Edict; that my failure to provide it before landing would subject me to a fine—only two dollars—and the securing of one in the city at the regular cost of issuance. As I knew this to be simply a means of robbing tourists, and unconstitutional in international law, I declined to pay the fine.

"You would hardly want to be imprisoned here, would you?" he asked. I confessed I wouldn't.

"I can not see any other way out, Mr. Spickler," he replied, "I will do what I can for you."

Tipping was more necessary in Constantinople than in most cities, but all I did was to hand out my picture and name. On it I crossed the famous Galata Bridge, entered museums and churches, and at the door of St. Sophia, where a charge of fifty cents was made, I handed the old door-keeper my picture, who looked at it upside down, handing it back to me with a wave of his arm to go on in. My visit to a Turkish graveyard one evening shocked me by its tatterdemalion looks. Not a stone was erect, many were flat on the ground, or in the act of falling. To increase their spectral gloom, some of them—the tombs of men—were crowned by the Turkish fez or cap, making them look like a petrified foot-ball team making a "touchdown." The Turk plants cypress trees near his grave, for he believes that the soul reposing beneath the slab, when drawn out of the grave by the little tuft of hair always left by barbers at the top of the shaven head for that purpose, may flit about in the shade of this tree, awaiting the judgment of the two angels who sit on each of the two caps covering the grave-stones. The souls of their women seem to have been unprovided in this way.

AROUND THE WORLD

One morning as I looked upon the Golden Horn, I wrote:

  "To be" is the world's grand verb,
   The words that thrill the blood.
  To me they come with subtle power,
   Or rush like mountain flood.

  "To shine" all the universe through,
   In youth of morning dawn,
  Is the God-like wish of every one,
   Though everything else be gone.

  "To love" is the world's best phrase,
   The ring that charms "to be."
  This is the span of the golden bridge
   That swings 'tween you and me.

Without a guide I set out to see the Sultan on his way for prayers at the Mosque, some miles from the hotel. In the lower city I lost sight of the Palace and got mixed up with some lattice-windowed harems. I was afraid to stop, and it was forbidden Europeans to inquire at these houses. Thousands of Moslem cavalry shot past me, their fleet Arab horses all but running over me, the bays, sorrels, browns, grays, and duns, running together. Some of these horsemen looked back at me, but not one of them smiled.

At last I reached the line of march, but at the wrong end. I took my stand behind the line, where two rows of men and one of horse guarded the road. But I was soon told to move up, and I was kept moving, until I reached the upper end where the great crowd had gathered. But I was to be the only non-Moslem among them. This excited the suspicions of the police, who came up to me, some of them jostling me as they passed to see if I carried any hidden weapon or bombs. I should have taken a guide, but he would have cost not only a fee, but also a conveyance, and I usually went about alone to save this expense. He would have taken me to another portion of the grounds where American

WITHOUT A CENT

and European tourists were grouped. When it was noised about that the Sultan was coming, one of these cops got in front of me and tried to push me back. But I hadn't risked my life getting there on the long run from the hotel to be thwarted in my plans to see the Sultan. I knew if he pushed me from my position at the front, I would be compelled to take a position on much lower ground, from which it would be next to impossible to get a glimpse of this arch-tyrant. A second cop fought his way through the mass to help this first one. But I stubbornly refused to move, and although they threatened, I made signs to them that I wanted to see their Ruler, and that I would then be willing to go wherever they wanted to take me. Then his carriage rolled slowly by, holding, like a prisoner of evil, Abdul Hamid, the woe-begone, brutal featured, licentious monarch of the Bloody Empire.

Three of them immediately surrounded me as if I were a wild beast. They were not accustomed to seeing one so different from themselves, in dress and looks, mixing in with them, in the Sultan's Gardens, and having already experienced my firmness to follow out my plans, they did not know what to expect from me when they came to arrest me. They were going through my pockets. The crowd was leaving the grounds, when a city-guide who had met me at the Bristol, stepped up and said the word that gave me my freedom.

The carriages were flying by with tourists and citizens returning to the European portion of Constantinople. I fell in behind one of these, reaching the hotel, five miles away, safely.

Back at the Consul's rooms I learned that my fine had been remitted. At these rooms was an Armenian refugee whose life was sought by the Turks, who had chased him through the city. Because of their lying in wait for him, he could not leave the American quarters, but had his meals brought in to him. When he told me how he had seen his friends and relatives

AROUND THE WORLD

tortured and put to death, you can imagine how I myself felt.

The blowing up a Turkish Transport, and the dynamiting of a train back of the city, with the dying and dead borne through the streets, urged my immediate leaving.

Back in Smyrna, where I had left my wheel, I asked first of all about the kitten. It had disappeared. Where it had gone, or how, the pupil could not tell, but he declared he had fed it, some time after I sailed. My mind went back to the court scene, and I wondered if in some distressing situation we should ever meet again.

OFF FOR THE HOLY LAND

The sea-ride from Smyrna to Joppa is one of the most inspiring excursions on the Globe. The Mediterranean, with its gentle zephyrs, its morning freshness, its many little islands rising like fascinating spectres out of the quiet blue, hugs a shore-line whose wild ways jag savage mountains that thrust their horny backs from blue above into blue below. The spicy mountain air came down, caressing the sea and ship with tender touch of sweetness.

    In scarlet plash of orange
    That paints the calm, blue sea
    With magic sweep of brush,
    I see the sun go down,
    Itself a ball of yellow gold,
    The standard unit of daylight skies.
And yonder glinted peaks, that rise
From out their sea-girt, purple thrones,
Wave to the sun their fondest "au revoir!"
    When it from me had gone.
So may some soaring angel o'er our earth,
When others turn away into their darksome night,
    By human axis governed,
Still wave to me a merry "Bon Voyage"
    When from me rolls
This dense dark globe of Night.

WITHOUT A CENT

Anchoring off Mersina, two miles out, in the morning, the Captain said he would lie here until twelve noon sharp. Tarsus, Paul's home town, was near here, so I was at once rowed ashore, caught the train on the little railroad managed by our Consul, and with fifteen minutes between trains to see Tarsus, I ran around the novel streets that wound up and unravelled at pleasure, kicking up ankle-deep dust, unable to find any one enough interested to show me Paul's birthplace, and listening for the down-coming train, which I soon heard, as it entered the yards a half mile away. Cutting corners, leaping stone walls, and grabbing at lemon and fig trees for souvenirs, I covered the distance just as the train began to move. On board was the Mayor of Tarsus, who gave me his signature. He warned me to hurry from the depot as soon as we stopped, if I meant to catch the ship, as there would be no time to spare. So when the train reached Mersina I sprinted for the wharf.

Smoke was rolling straight up from the funnels of the steamer as I jumped into a row-boat and urged the Arab to make quick strokes for the same, with hardly thirty minutes left in which to do it, when an arrogant Turkish cop laid his hand upon me, and ordered the boatman to tie up, took my Passport, and commanded me to follow him.

In several languages I tried to tell him, and I gestured in more, how necessary it was that I catch this ship by twelve o'clock. But he paid no attention to what I was trying to tell him, and kept on taking me back from the wharf into the Turkish town. I pleaded with him. I pressed his arm gently. I almost cried. But he kept on going away from the wharf. I called to him, but he only twisted his neck contemptuously, making fun of my painful dilemma. Then I ran ahead of him, begging him to increase his pace so that we might somehow be able to get back from where he meant to take me, and still by some good fortune, reach the vessel before she sailed away with my wheel, valuable papers, and luggage.

Fifteen minutes had gone. In fifteen more the boat would sail. It would take thirty minutes to be rowed out to her, but I meant to try to get there, if only he would let me go now. Then he led me into a building before an officious snob, told him something about me, while I stood a prisoner before him. That rascal threw up his Moslem hands and waved me to another officer, blocks farther back, through littered courts and crooked passageways where lay scores of roughnecks. My buoyant enthusiasm, so increased by my having seen Paul's birthplace, and getting back in time to make the train, and then the ship, was all spoiled by this Satanic Imp of Mahomet, who had clouded the rest of my journey by his uncalled for deviltry.

At the edge of a wall he led me into a room where a third dignitary was at lunch. The man was enjoying his meal, so without waiting for the cop to speak to him, I began the talk myself. He told him to let me go, gesturing the words so that I also might understand what he had said. The cop, like a coward, then motioned me to go away, if I liked, still holding my Passport, and knowing full well the difficulties I would have finding my way back to the wharf. Taking me part way, he was about to hand me my Passport, and to let me go on alone, when a new idea seemed to strike his mind. Glutting his appetite for more tyranny, and treating me as if I were his criminal prisoner, so that natives might scorn me or attack me, he was deliberating, when to my encouraged surprise, the United States Consul, just then crossing the end of the street, saw me in the hands of this mock Justice. He came to my rescue ordering him to free me.

When we finally reached the front street I was most happily surprised to see the "Lazareff" still at anchor. She had been delayed by extra cargo. A

WITHOUT A CENT

second boatman secured, my Passport delivered me. I now had hopes of reaching her before she sailed. If I did so, I meant to pay the rower twice the regular fee, but on the way out he demanded his fee. Tourists are warned not to pay this until they are landed, or otherwise they are made to pay a second or even a third fee. Of all my boatmen he was the most savage and importunate, as well as the biggest and the strongest. But the more importunate he was to get his fee before he had earned it, so much more persistent was I not to pay it. I had won the other case. I meant to win this. We were nearing the boat, in a heavy sea, and with my camera in my mouth I was about to leap into the water and swim, when a wave struck us and dashed us right against the flying steps, when I made a jump for them, and drew myself up on deck. When he came up for his pay I handed him his legal fare.

The next morning we sailed into Beirut at the foot of the Lebanons. I fairly danced with joy when I saw our two American battleships lying here in the harbor, their guns trained on the city in defense of the American College, now threatened by the Moslems for rapine and plunder. A Turkish boatman rowed me to the "San Francisco."

When ready to return to the "Lazareff" the Captain placed me into his little launch, the Stars and Stripes flying at the stern, kissing the blue Mediterranean and flinging back defiance at tyranny as she glided past the Turkish boats. And when I climbed the rope ladder my voyage companions from northern ports leaned over the taft rail to get a closer glimpse of the little American launch and of the able Yankees managing her, and when I stepped on deck again they took me by the hand with such an enthusiastic fervor as to make me feel that to be just a plain American citizen was a fortune in itself!

When nearing Joppa the Russian Jews aboard bound square little boxes called "frontlets" to their foreheads, the leather thongs passing around the head, and then tied. On the left arm they wrapped a leather strap in seven twists, after which they twisted their bodies in fantastic shapes while reciting parts of the Old Testament, in preparation for landing in the Holy Land, the most wonderful event in their lives, and in mine.

Five big Arabs rowed me and wheel ashore, apparently not caring to take any other passenger in their big boat, and asking me only about one-fourth regular fare, which I voluntarily doubled when I saw how hard it was to row me safely over the sunken rocks.

My first five minutes in Joppa was worth a thousand a minute. How strange the customs! I went up the hilly, crooked streets in the hot afternoon, buying watermelon, oranges, figs, and other fruits raised in Joppa. Our Lord chose a good country in which to be born. My tires were in bad shape and as I was eager to get my mail so as to know if mother was alive, I boarded the little train for Jerusalem! Sixty miles of emotion! I was out on the platform most of the way, for weren't we to go through the Plain of Sharon, and didn't I want to see everything, including the eagles soaring high above the mountains? As the train puffed up the steep grade near the Holy City I pulled a ripe fig from a tree growing close to the track as I stood on the lower step of the platform. Then, as the train reached the top of the Judean Hills at early evening, some one cried: "That's Jerusalem!" When it stopped a half mile outside the walls the natives who had come to the depot to greet friends leaped at them like madmen, kissing them first on one cheek, then on the other, men with men. Cook's Agency, where my mail had been forwarded, was closed for the day, so I could not get it until the morrow. Mother had been carried to the hospital. No one believed she would live. Her last message reached me in Ireland just before she

WITHOUT A CENT

went under the knife. So the letter that lay in the Tourist Office had news that would make me glad or sad beyond words. From the roof of the Grand Hotel I asked to be shown, first of all, Calvary, then Mount Olive.

That night I slept in Jerusalem!

With arms full of mail in the morning I ran to the Hotel to open it. First the letters from home, in the order of post-marked dates. But before them, the one from the hospital that contained the news that caused my trembling hands to hurry. Her nurse had written it. She said she believed my mother would pull through! The next letter said that she was about to leave the hospital! I never before knew the full value of "good news from a far country." But to get such news in the Holy Land! And in mother's own hand, as the next letter was.

The Holy Land could now unroll for me in fairest colors beneath my buoyant spirits. I was to have a grand time, and I knew it. I went about the city like one enchanted. Tourists at the hotel were happier because of my joy. At the Pool of Bethesda I bathed my temples, my eyes and my lips, and recalling mother's sweet voice as she sang "By Cool Siloam's Shady Rill," I sought this spot, hoping that its olden balm might make my eyes to see more of the goodness of this world, and that my lips, anointed with this seraphic spring might speak more effectively the praise of my Maker. None but the real Christian can know the delight and emotion, so strangely wonderful, that filled my soul when for the first time I looked upon these most sacred spots on earth. It was so easy to bow the head and say grace at the table, to kneel and say my evening prayer, there where Jesus had been! It was good just to get into bed and fall asleep, and then to waken, in the night, or in the morning, and remember that I was in the most wonderful of all cities. Over everything and in everything I saw the Christ, with customs and habits

AROUND THE WORLD

the same as in the days of Abraham and Joseph. I saw the wheat heaped in the measure, then pressed down, shaken together, and finally heaped up again, as it ran over on all sides, when it was poured "into the bosom" which was the big loose, sacklike folds of the outer garment above the belt. I want to be so full of life I can't help running over, for others.

Near the "Place of a Skull" outside the Wall, the gardener caring for the Tomb refused to take a single penny when he knew I had started penniless. No pomp or ornamentation was there to create a false impression. It was still an "unfinished," that is, a "new" tomb. The vault cut in the solid rock was about seven feet square, the right side below the little window being the portion meant for an adult.

Jerusalem is still a big city where it is hard to find your way. When I visited the Temple Area, Dr. Merrill, our noble Consul, furnished me a Kwas or guide to represent the United States, the Turkish Government furnished a soldier to represent Turkey, and I had my own personal guide to represent me. In this official state I was conducted also to the Mosque of the Sacred Stone, being compelled to remove my shoes before entering where the sacred fire burned the sacrifices. I touched it. The temple had gone, as Jesus said it would go, without one stone upon another. That same afternoon I walked out to Gethsemane, a beautiful flower-garden now maintained by an American lady.

Midnight Walk to Jericho

The most dangerous journey was my midnight walk, alone, unarmed, to Jericho. When I left my hotel in Jerusalem at five in the evening I expected to reach the Samaritan Inn, ten miles away, before dark. It was not my intention to make a night journey of it, when the peril from Syrian robbers is greatest. But I lost my way, and when I found St. Stephen's Gate, the sun was low.

WITHOUT A CENT

The Brook Kedron, gorging the rough valley flanking the eastern wall, lay below me. Beyond it, half way up Mount Olive, on the left, Gethsemane. Passing Absalom's Tomb on my right, the road swings in a grand half-circle around the southern slope of the Mount. In the side of the hill was the traditional spot where Judas took his life. Beyond, near the road, the site of the fig-tree cursed by the Master. Several miles around, Bethany.

"A certain man went down to Jericho." If he went at all, he went down. One thousand feet fall in twenty miles is great. This is four thousand! Although the stars were now out, revealing the forms of the mountains beneath their beams, the light failed to penetrate the deep canyons. It was easy to imagine every black object a ghoul and moving.

No one goes alone over this road. The Bedouins themselves are afraid to do it. No other tourist had ever made the night journey alone. Two weeks before, two fellahin, at the point of guns, were ordered to give up their valuables and clothing, and then were made to ride off into the desert. The Saviour's "certain man" was first stripped and then beaten.

The road led up through a deep cut that flung itself around a jutting cliff. Here, on the left, a feeble light flickered from the open door of a low building. It was the Samaritan Inn. And I was half way down.

The landlord urged me to stay till morning. He told me of hyenas that prowled at night. Of wolves, wild-cats and panthers; of hundreds of robbers I would meet.

So I paid for my lodging and was shown into another room occupied by some wild looking men upon the floor and on cots.

I knelt and prayed as was my custom, threw myself upon the hard cot, mechanically crossed my hands and became a formal candidate for sleep. But I soon found that a mind churned by such extraordinary excitement refused to be quieted. Then it was that an enemy more numerous and irritating than all the brigands made an unexpected sally from their hiding-place. The sting of the fleas, added to the sting of cowardice for stopping here insulted my Yankee grit. I wondered if the wounded man, carried here two thousand years before me, had to endure these awful pests. I was mad that I had paid for lodging I could not use, and at midnight came out to see the landlord for a second time.

When I came out into the office there stood before me three of the most typical wild Bedouins I had seen. The first look of their shiny, black eyes, set in dark faces two-thirds hidden by blankets to their feet, was suggestive of treachery. But I was mad at the fleas, and danger seemed attractive in comparison.

"They are going to Jericho on camels," said he, as their piercing eyes ran over me in search of booty, "they will show you the way."

I was between two fires, the fleas and the robbers. Their looks—the wildest picture of humanity I ever saw, and at midnight, on the road to Jericho, cooled my pedestrian ardor.

Jericho is near the Jordan. The Jordan is the boundary between the land of Moab and the Holy Land. The Bedouins of Moab are to the Bedouins of the Holy Land as outlaw desperadoes are to civilized robbers. Regular tourists never wander into the land beyond the Jordan, and the daring adventurer who risks his life to penetrate that wild and lawless region must be accompanied by a heavy guard of Turkish soldiery. Wonder not therefore at my fright when the landlord told me that these thieves were from the east of the Jordan! I shall never forget the full force of that phrase. So I hesitated. They were leaving the Inn. As the last one passed out he waved me to follow, uttering something in Arabic that would have made a baby cry. I wondered what I should do. To go to Jericho with a party of outlaws was paradoxical.

WITHOUT A CENT

But I was unwilling to return to the fleas, and I knew these men could not be trusted.

Drawn by a strange fascination I slowly followed into the moonless night. Once outside, the men began to mount big camels, having them first kneel on the stony road. One begged me to get on in front of him.

"No!" I said, by gesture and voice, "I'll walk!" At least I wouldn't ride with a Bedouin behind me!

When the three camels moved off tandem, with me following the heels of the last one, I was dumbfounded to find fifty or more others join us in the darkness. I hadn't planned for these, so I hung back. The men on the camels, seeing me trying to slip away from them, stopped their camels, calling to me, and starting again when I came up to them. I had to go, the longest ten miles I ever walked, and the most perilous.

Thinking to compel me to ride, their camels were urged into a brisk trot. But the idea of running was attractive to me, for it would sooner bring an end to my suspense. We passed in close succession three caravans, mostly of donkeys, whose drivers, seeing me tagging behind the camels, asked the men who I was and how they captured me!

After a time the third Bedouin dropped back as if to join the crowd we were fast leaving behind, to bribe them, I suppose, to keep silence if any harm should befall me at the hands of the two men left with me. Of the two remaining ones I chose the one whose camel and voice I less feared. My first duty was to get so well acquainted with voice and camel that in losing him while mixing in the up-coming caravans, I could easily find him again. So I pressed his bare foot and slapped his leg.

Suddenly, while passing through a narrow gorge, the camels were brought to a halt, turned at right angles to the road and commanded to kneel, uttering loud bawls of unwillingness in which I silently joined.

They had selected a spot most desolate. For a moment my head swam in the light ether above me. But poise reasserted itself, and with it, courage. They seemed to change their mind, and I was merely asked to get on and ride, which I refused.

"Get on behind!" he said.

Still I refused.

If I rode they might demand a fee, take my camera and clothes for pay, or possibly make me a prisoner, and hurry me across the Jordan, where they would hold me for ransom. When at last they started I helped my friend into his hunch-back saddle. As I helped him on, my hands recoiled as they touched a sword, dagger and pistol concealed under his blanket.

Twice I was frightened. The two Bedouins, with their long-legged camels, had out-traveled the herd of donkeys which require rest every mile or so. We were again alone. Suddenly they stopped short and listened, leaning far out over their camels' necks. They knew how far behind we had left our own caravan. It was for any who might be coming up from below they listened. I knew they had planned something in which I was to figure.

We had descended on the road so far as to suffer from oppression of the atmosphere below sea-level. A sultry calm hung with gloomy pallor over the herbless hills. The Bedouins now left the road where a level waste lay between the two wadies. I hung behind until they halted. They had dismounted and driven the camels off to graze upon thorn bushes, evidently intending to take plenty of time for their scheme. Their blankets or outer garments were then spread upon the sand. Upon these they laid their weapons, all save a dagger in the belt of the one on my left, which he did not believe I had seen. Each then squatted upon the blankets, bidding me to sit between them. I sat, but not for rest, far enough from each robber to make an equilateral triangle between us, ready to spring to my feet in an instant. While

WITHOUT A CENT

the one on my right tried to get my attention on the sword he was bending double, the one on my left slowly slided behind me. So I kept moving, too, to maintain the proper distance from him. There in the glittering starlight lay their weapons. Here we three sat, at two in the morning, with no law to govern us but the law of the desert. I knew they meant to spring some trick to overpower me. I had only one weapon, a western mind (and the Master who walked the same road), so I watched each man as a hawk watches the gunner.

Then they argued together. By accent and gesture I knew about what they said.

"Shall we do it?"

"No!"

"Why not?"

"He may explode that thing on us!" (the camera).

For a minute they were silent—the longest of my life.

Then they arose, took up their weapons and blankets, called their camels and were off. Again I refused to ride, saying that as Jericho was so near, I preferred to walk.

Soon we came to the edge of the hills. Before us, in the coming dawn, lay the sandy brown plain, the road curving carelessly over the gray dunes and across the rough bed of a dry stream. Yonder, dimly blue, rose the mountains of Moab, where Ruth lived.

The last tryst with the thieves was about a mile from Jericho, where as before, we sat on the blankets. This time, however, they retained their weapons in their belts, and I knew by their actions they meant to rob me. The lunch I carried was to keep me alive along the Jordan, but I decided to give it up rather than lose everything, for it is a law of the desert that he who eats with these Bedouins shall be saved from harm.

"Dog!" I said, the Arabic word for "eat," handing them my lunch of sausage and sandwiches. They began to "dog" the pork sausage forbidden them by their religion, smacking their lips as if it were young chicken. Dawn was streaking the east. Pointing to the morning star I made signs that we be off at once. Half an hour later one flung his bony arm in the direction of a faint light, crying:

"Er Riha! Saba-jal-sof-keloama!" (Jericho! There is your hotel.)

Their camels were then urged into a fast trot towards the Fords of the Jordan.

When I told of my night's adventure with the Bedouins, Hotel Belle Vue made me their guest.

The sun was already scorching the hot sands shimmering in tremulous heat waves over the flat waste, when I set out for the Jordan four miles away. The risk I was taking alone, to see it, made it all the more interesting, as I penetrated the dense woodland on the bank, when I suddenly came right upon it—a little stream like a swollen creek, where I took a swim in its swift current and then a little boat ride, rowing across and touching the Land of Moab with my fingers, so I might add that country to my travels! In places the channel was only about thirty feet wide, in others as much as one hundred and fifty. I picked my way along for five miles, thrilled by the wildness of the place and by the sacred memories. A big gray wolf crossed just ahead of me; then, armed with a revolver, a naked wild Bedouin planted himself squarely in my path, both of which tamed my zeal of floundering alone in this jungle, and made me hurry away.

On the second day I walked six miles over the desert where the yellow dust went whirling in the slightest breeze in this rainless valley, while the fine sand squirted out from under every step like burning embers, to the Dead Sea on which I could float, my head on my arms for a pillow, until I had to shriek for pain that the slimy, acrid water gave me when it got into my eyes, and raw places of the skin. In

WITHOUT A CENT

this predicament a woman emerged from a little shack back from the beach and set a pail of sweet water at a safe distance.

After wandering around the site of old Jericho, where not even a stone of the wall can be seen, drinking from a big pool of spring water, I walked back to Jerusalem, even more afraid than when I came down. For three days I was ill with the heat and excitement, and Jerusalem was talking of my rare adventure.

With a Moslem guide, Strubel, I left Jerusalem by the Damascus Gate for a long walk north. We took our first lunch under an olive tree on the old caravan route btween Egypt and Damascus, carrying little flat loaves, and depending on vineyards and orchards when towns were scarce. Mountainous all day, we reached a narrow gorge, dreaded by tourists and called the "Robber's Spring," at sunset, which Strubel declined to enter, drawing his hand across his throat to indicate its reputation. Much against his will I urged him on. At the bottom of the valley we drank from the deep spring from which the Master must often have drank. On the other side, Bedouins were eating supper in their camp. If we stopped near them they would trouble us during the night, so I made Strubel follow me right into their camp, the natives looking at us, bewildered. Putting down my bundle I began to eat my supper, Strubel doing the same. One by one they came up to me, trying to talk, and ending by prying into my pockets. Refused this privilege, one of their number with fine face rebuked them, when most of them stood back. My guide still wondered at my audacity, for of all parties he had guided he seemed to say to me that no one had shown such downright bravado before. But it was the best thing I could do, to trust them as my hosts. Two of them persisted in feeling around my clothes for valuables, when they were severely reprimanded by him.

Taking a chance, I smoothed out the sand, and fell

asleep. It must have been about two o'clock when I was awakened by something being pressed to my lips and a pair of long legs standing over me. The moon had sunk behind the mountain-wall, but I could see the forms of several others near by. My first thought was that I was being robbed, when I sat up and received into my hands a big bunch of juicy grapes, which he and his mates had foraged.

Near Jacob's well a woman and her daughter asked me for "backsheesh," which I refused, when they seized my staff and refused to return it until I had tipped both, for you can possibly get along here without money, but you must have your staff for protection. At high noon we reached the Well, just as did the Saviour, and I sat, as he did, tired, thirsty and hungry, on the low curb, quenching our thirst with water, not from the dry well, seventy-five feet deep, but from a cistern. The water that did me the most good was the kind Jesus spoke of here. Passing into Samaria between the two high hills, Gerizim and Ebal, children rudely followed us down one of the only two streets, and they parallel, in the town of twenty springs, and several hundred Samaritans who look for Christ the first time, in six thousand years.

The third day we came to the threshing-floor of Abraham, where the woman-dressed farmer threshed his grain with young cows and piled the wheat on the bare ground. Not far away we came to a spring which my guide said was poisonous, as were numerous other ones. He had been in the habit of drinking before I drank, and finally, at the last spring, he had washed his face in it, ending up by washing his feet, before I had drank. As he was doing this, I grabbed him by the neck and threw him aside, threatening damage to his looks if he ever did it again. Near Dothan, where Joseph was sold, we lunched under a fig-tree, and in it, for the keeper sitting below it, let me climb up in it and eat all I wanted for a metelik—one cent.

WITHOUT A CENT

Bedouin Courtship

In the camp a boy may see a girl he fancies, when he shows her his affection by speaking to her more politely than to another, and he may offer to carry something for her; or he may walk with her from one tent to another, fifteen to fifty feet, but they must not go out of sight. Courting would help neither party. The main consideration is money. The father seldom parts with a girl for less than two hundred and fifty dollars, or its equivalent in five cows, some sheep and a donkey. A donkey is always included. The man who can pay this amount gets the girl. The question of love or taste finds no place in the bargain. Girls are married in their twelfth and thirteenth year, and pretty ones often at ten. A boy and girl about eleven were herding cows. She was his wife, and she was enceinte. At Jericho a little boy was to have been married to a little girl at a certain hour. He couldn't see any sense in it. So he ran away, and was found playing marbles. No lover is sure of his bride even after he buys her. At least half of the money must be paid down before delivery of goods, and sometimes the father will raise the price after receiving this amount, especially if she be good looking, or talented.

The groom does the inviting, to his house or tent, for the wedding, the men coming by themselves, and the women likewise. Then they dance, the men with men, the women with women, until late at night. Then the groom serves all with a tiny cup of coffee-grounds, when they depart, those from a distance being allowed to sleep under the same tent or out on the bare ground, or even on the roof of the house, if they have one. The next day, or soon after, the groom and bride go to the mosque, followed by the people in informal procession, where the sheik or muezzin reads that portion of the Koran relating to marriage, after which the girls take the bride, the boys the groom, to the groom's house, which is a new tent, or a corner of the old one, of his father. They may dance again, after which all squat on the ground, when the hat is passed for a collection, each donation being called out in a loud voice, as "Nahum Sebuk, ten cents,' "Ximal Bilky, five cents," the wealthier giving as high as fifty cents, which call for loud cheers. Then comes the supper, the marriage supper referred to by Jesus, prepared by the groom's family, and all in one big dish, first, a layer of bread with soup poured over it, then a layer of rice, over which is placed a layer of roast mutton or beef. The dish is set in the middle of the floor, when the guests hurriedly gather around it, the men, of course, leading, and the others, men and women, next to these, each one's face close to the back of the one next, when they eat of the meat and rice, handing out small portions to those out of reach of the dish, the outer ones sometimes getting no meat, and but little rice. These finish the bread. Coffee is served in little cups, three or four sufficing for the whole number. Then the groom gives the hint that the time for leaving has come. If they do not go at once, he takes more forcible means.

He is then alone with his bride. After the marriage privilege he leaves her for a moment and fires a pistol in the air to let the village know that another family has been added to the community. The "best" man hangs around the tent until the firing, when he shouts aloud to their health. The next day, the groom, having prepared another feast, for the same guests, goes about the village, crying: "Come! All things are ready!"

An old maid is a girl eighteen to twenty. No one wants her. That is why her father sells his daughter so young. He is sure of his money.

These Bedouin travel about much like gypsies, and they are fully as ready to increase their prosperity, by one means or another. Some of them were hard to get rid of, and the party with the greatest number of

WITHOUT A CENT

fighting men usually wins out. I found out a plan which always prevented trouble, providing it could be used. On meeting these desert folk I always saw to it that I bade them the time of the day, first, before they had spoken to me, when they would politely return the compliment, without stopping us. I would say:

"Naharak sa-id!" (Blessed good day.) And they would answer:

"Naharak mubarak!" (Yours be blessed) most deferentially.

When they treated me to coffee or water in the desert, I said:

"Diama!" (Thanks.)

"Beti betak!" they replied. (My house belongs to you.)

On entering the Valley of Jezreel, I was glad to find a village in which a prosperous Moslem received guests into his house, so that for one night at least there would be no wild animals or roving bands of thieves to molest us. Fried chicken was served for supper, and lemonade was made from water taken from a pool in which the ducks swam, the dog waded, and the horse drank. That night we were all trying to sleep on top of the house, the men at one end, the women at the other, fighting mosquitoes, when we heard cries from below. From the edge of the roof we could see the father giving his two boys a cold bath in this same pool, holding them down under the water, their lusty yells rousing the other guests, who wrapped in white sheets and moonlight looked like spectres craning their necks over the wall.

"Just think!" said one of the feminines, "and our lemonade came from that hole!"

In the morning I counted three hundred bites by Moslem mosquitoes over my body—mosquitoes hatched from that pool. With quinine and ammonia I fought the fever off for weeks, for typhus raged in that town.

AROUND THE WORLD

I turned aside to see an Arab Tournament by Gibeon's Fountain, where young men did fancy riding at the edge of the probable town in which Jesus raised the only son to life, each wearing calico dresses, carrying old pistols that threatened not to stay cocked, and long muskets that went off in most any direction. The men then danced in a small circle, by threes and fours, swinging by a center man who thought he was playing a rude reed piccolo, the men humming a jargon and setting their feet down with rather pretty effect, shouting and leaping wildly at intervals. I knew the dislike of these men to have their pictures taken, so I tried to get a "snap" without their knowing it. Some one saw me do it, when they all broke from the ring and surrounded me. With the dollar or so that I carried, I could not frank the crowd, so I backed away, tossing a metelik in their midst, hurrying away as they struggled to find it. Yelling and cursing, fifteen or twenty followed, seizing me, when one of them pointed his cocked pistol at my head, as the others began to fumble my pockets. With a quick sweep of my hand I brushed the gun aside and shamed them for attacking one so defenseless, when the leader called them off, my guide offering me no assistance whatever, and hoping I would be robbed that he might come in for his share, a rule followed by these guides. After I hurried away, the men mounted their horses and dashed after me, but for some reason, changed their mind, wheeled and flew back, their little horses bending and turning under them with the fury of untamable wildness.

>Nazareth, thy streets are holy walks,
> Thy dust is precious gold;
>Thy caverns and thy faded rocks
> Are fair as stories told.

"Ta'al bukra daha sa'a arba' unuss!" I said to my guide, in Nazareth, the evening before we set out

WITHOUT A CENT

for the Sea of Galilee, the longest sentence I ever tried on him. (Come to me tomorrow morning at half past four o'clock, for Galilee.) "Na'am," he replied, and clogged down the steps from the hotel.

At Cana's only water supply, the spring at the edge of town, beautifully dressed women bearing large jars on their heads and shoulders, came and went in a constant stream. Resting here awhile, we took up our journey for the lake, lying between tan-colored, russet-hued mountains, six hundred and eighty-one feet below the sea, one of the prettiest bodies of water on the earth. A French lady invited me to join her in a boat-ride across the lake, on Sunday morning, a wonderful excursion, and one of the best sermons I ever saw, and twelve miles long. Our little ship was a row and sail boat like Peter's, with four big Arabs at the long oars.

> Sea of Galilee, enchanted,
> Where the Saviour's feet were planted.
> Magic lake of waters blue,
> I am sailing now on you.

The lake rolled at first, but soon fell into a glassy smoothness, so that I could read my little Bible, when the New Testament became as real to me as a letter from home. Jesus, as the preacher that morning, told us that Capernaum would be utterly thrown down. We passed Magdala to Capernaum's ruin.

With a hook and line made from a horse-hair I fished in the lake on Monday with no more success than Peter enjoyed before Christ came to him, but I could see hundreds of fish gliding around my hook. Three times I went swimming in the lake, and as it is fifty to five hundred feet deep, I did not wade much.

In an old synagogue at Tiberias I was taken up into the pulpit, and at my request the Book of Genesis was delivered to me, from which I read, in the old Hebrew, "In the beginning, God——" the graybeards looking on in puzzled wonder, faces beaming, glad that a hiking tourist could read the Bible in their own tongue.

While waiting for "coffee" in the Carmel House in Haifa on the Mediterranean, a town half Moslem, and many Germans, I dashed off twelve lines which I sold to a patriotic soap-maker.

> Fairest town in all the land,
>   Verdant Haifa by the sea;
> Bright with shells upon thy strand,
>   Haifa, gay and full of glee.
> Set in groves of graceful trees,
>   Olive, byzerine, and palm,
> Odors sweet are in thy breeze,
>   Life, and joy, and healing balm.
> Haifa, on thy crescent Bay
>   At the foot of Carmel green,
> Take from me my simple lay,
>   Let me call thee Syria's Queen!

On Mount Carmel I found with some hazard the spot thought to have been the Baal Altar, where I built one of twelve stones, descending from the tangled brush and scrub-oak to the Brook Kishon full of water, through Druse villages to Zammarin, where wind-mills, fertile fields, grazing herds, and good roads, made this Hebrew-German settlement an oasis. Ill with the fever begun on the housetop, I asked for some hot water, but was refused by the Jews, because it was their Sabbath, and they said they could not sell anything on Sunday. I did not want them to go to hell for selling me a little hot water. They could give it to me. One was so tickled to hear me speak Hebrew, he went away and told everybody that a stranger was in town who could speak seven languages.

"We are not running a hotel," was the arrogant answer of a German in his home.

HOLY LAND

Bearing Water Jar to Cana Springs

Author Viewing Sacred Rock in Stocking Feet—Temple Area

HOLY LAND AND CEYLON

WITHOUT A CENT

Then a young German with two chums came along, who asked me all about my tour. I was too weak to talk much, but believing it might win the needed hot water, I endured the pain, barely able to stand, when I told him I was decidedly ill and would like to have a little hot water.

"I must go and pray," replied the fellow, in good English.

"Will you come to me afterwards?" I then asked.

"Yes, I'll be back soon. I must go to church now and pray."

Two hours passed. People were going to bed. Two plain Arabs were eating a late supper on the ground near us. These men understood, and without my asking, these gentlemen of the desert set out for me two dishes of steaming hot food, which they had cooked there on a litle fire, refusing the money I offered them. This hot nourishment, part soup and part solid, cured me almost instantly. "When were you hungry, or thirsty, or naked, or in prison?" "A cup of (hot) water!" Then I laid down on the ground and waited all night for the praying hypocrite.

The next morning we walked to Caesarea and boarded a little sailing vessel for Joppa, thirty miles down. In the high wind our vessel lay on her side, and was dripping water, when a canvas was stretched along the side and securely fastened. On the way the men tried to exact three times the rate agreed upon, waving their fists in front of us, and all but striking us in their fiery demonstrations of bullying. But this did not take all the fun out of the sail, and the charm and uncertainty of being swamped at sea, miles from land, added to the excitement of the voyage.

On a path bleak and wild, we started at sunset for the city, trying to sleep on the ground but troubled by scores of howling wolves.

At noon we began climbing the mountains, bleak but grand, that are around about Jerusalem.

I had walked three hundred miles. Often in my walks I could see the entire land in one grand sweep of vision. Just as if I had come up to attend it, the Feast of Tabernacles was going on. My home was in a Jewish family of five girls and boys, for I wanted to live awhile with the "Chosen People." As I sat at the table with the family I imagined the time of the old Bible characters. My breakfasts were brought to my little room by one of the girls. One morning I went with the father to the Synagogue, where everybody walked about the church with their hats on, in time of service, amid the greatest confusion, every one praying out loud from the Old Testament, ducking their heads forward and in circles, the Chief Pharisee of them all up in the reading desk, acting more ridiculously than any others. The church was lighted by dirty oil lamps. No art was visible, and the one important feature of any religious service, the women, was shut off by a lattice in the balcony, and few young people were present to stimulate these pious anachronisms.

INTO EGYPT. "MASTER" OF THE SHIP

Having heard of my adventures over the Holy Land, the Khedival Line, inerested in my plans, handed me a free ticket, my first and only free ocean ride. Armed with this compliment of their recognition, I was rowed out over the violently washed rocks by five athletic Arabs to the S. S. Dahkalie, for Egypt.

As my pass did not call for meals or berth, I was making my rude bed of ropes and canvas at dusk, when a sailor came up, and said:

"The Captain wants to see you, sir, in First Cabin."

I followed along the slanting deck, puzzled as to his motive in sending for me. He met me at the door of First Cabin, talked a few moments with me, then asked me to come in and take a seat at the table, introducing me to his wife and daughter, now being served soup as the first course of the splendid meal.

WITHOUT A CENT

From that moment I was their guest, and when I left, I was asked to come in for all of my meals!

I was rejoicing with feelings unutterably grateful while putting the finishing touches to my bed of ship's rope, as I looked eagerly forward to taking my meals in the First Cabin, when the Captain himself came up to me, saying:

"Come with me!"

I thought maybe he had regretted asking me to come into his presence for my meals, and I followed him in doubt as to what he was about to do. He took me into his elegant state rooms, three ensuite, as if to show me the superb equipment, the nautical instruments, the chic bath-room, and the luxurious bed. As he left me, he said:

"You may occupy my headquarters during the voyage. Be at home here. Read the magazines, take a bath, or do what you like. When ready to sleep, there is my bed of clean linen for you. I'm going down with my family."

Without waiting for me to recover my senses to make a suitable reply, he was gone. I could hardly have been more surprised if he had turned his commission as Captain over to me, which in a way, he had done, for there were the signal buttons:

"Full Speed," "Reverse Engines," "Man Overboard," "Fire on Deck," any one of which I could have pushed.

I began at once to enjoy everything, by sitting on the soft cushions, walking over the fluffy rugs, looking into the compass as its jewelled needle quivered on its pivot, looked out of the Captain's "Squint," to see if all was well on deck, and over the sea; took a hot bath, then a cold douche; drank of the iced mineral water; wrote my notes out on the polished table under brilliant electric light; read again the story of Joseph, and crawled in between soft merino blankets, glad that the Captain had "forsaken all and cleaved unto his wife." The suite of rooms amidships, high up on the first deck, was worth, if they could be rented en-voyage, one hundred dollars a day.

For a side-trip I took a fast train to Cairo, fifty miles along the Suez Canal, then into the awful desert, and out again into a most fertile plain of Indian corn, big bunches of ripening dates hanging high on palms, while Egyptian farmers plowed, planted and cultivated, harvested and marketed, at the same time, planting the seed from boats, in the mud below the overflowed Nile. Crossing the Nile on a ferry I was soon on the back of a camel in the Libyan Desert, where like great clouds of smoke, the simmering simoon rolled over the vast vault of death, making me shudder at the thought of my camel breaking off into the limitless lure of billowy banks of sand. It was the last of October, yet the sun burned its beams through my clothing, and blistered my skin. The Sphinx did not appeal to me. But the great Pyramid was worth entering, as with candle I followed the Sheik by the tortuous channel to the very heart of it, where in the old sarcophagus of Pharaoh I laid down.

Back at Port Said I caught a French Liner for Ceylon, crossing the Red Sea where the waters parted to aid the Lord's people, and came together again to destroy their enemies, with Sinai in the distance, hundreds of flying-fish rising out of the water by our side, flying a quarter to a half mile, and then, as if hating to do so, dropping back into the water. Because I could talk a little Greek, the Greek pastryman fed me with baked sweets, and the Chinese frappe-man took me down six floors to the ship's refrigerator, where I helped him make ice cream, eating a dish or two to see if it was all right.

IN FRAGRANT CEYLON

We landed at Colombo, on the wonder-filled island of Ceylon, where I registered with scores of other passengers at the Grand, having about enough money in my pocket to buy a sandwich. My travels had

WITHOUT A CENT

taught me that I was a Bank, myself, and when I needed cash, I drew, on myself. This is the only bank that never fails, the only one with unlimited resources. Its cash deposits are greater than that of the First National, and its doors never close. Like anything else, you must have faith in it. But more than all else, you must draw on it. About the worst calamity that can overtake the average person is to lose their pocket-book, or become "broke" far from home. But my joy was just as exquisite when in London I found myself with nine pennies in my pocket, as when in Naples I had gold and to spare for my sea passage on a beautiful steamer for a two weeks' cruise. If I have no boat or train to catch, with plenty of time, I do not worry when without funds, whether a mile, or a million, from home. I simply plan a way, to earn my way, and get away.

After tiffin, or lunch, I rode over the strange city, and out into the jungle, every inch a veritable fairyland of human and physical curiosities. Though very hot, it was still very agreeable. No speech, no gesture, no exclamation can come within a thousand miles of telling just what you see, and how you feel, in this supreme circus-land. The air is different, the noises soft and sweet, mellow and soothing, lulling with undertones and overtones of dreamy weirds, enthralling with spells of romance that hang the hours, like golden gems, about the lovely neck of Day. Reverence, steeped in ages of religious devotion, customs and habits, boiled down to the concentrated essence of the bizarre, greet you with profound respect for themselves, the brilliant array of multi-moving manners amid the flashing landscape, entirely new to you, enthralling and enthusing. Gorgeous palms rose everywhere, singly and in groves, all kinds and shapes, tinged with the most delicate of greens, hiding bowered homes amid strange flowers and foliage. Countless throngs came and went, right in the street, making me dismount to avoid collision, every man wearing a bright red or blue parasol or a **ruffle about** his thigh. Big bare-legged men with only a breech-cloth ran wildly about, pulling after them two-wheeled rickshaws holding one or more natives or tourists, like children at play; and when men were not hitched up, cows were.

In the suburbs I came upon a native funeral procession headed by a jungle band, the corpse a woman, in sitting posture, borne on the heads of four young men in a sort of landau adorned with cheese cloth, strings of pop-corn and candy, the dead wife and mother riding as if to her coronation. Behind came the black husband, a colored towel about his thighs, carrying his little boy. As the musicians played and danced in a circle, the people fell in line behind.

It seemed that I had landed in a different world, and at first I was afraid of these queer people. The men took turn in digging the grave, after which incense was burned at the side, when the body was taken into the arms of one and handed down to two men in the grave. Then a relative jumped in and stripped it of all ornaments, from legs, toes, arms and face. A few pennies were then tossed into the grave, with some candy and fruit for her to eat on the way.

At supper three old men as waiters, in white dresses, with hair done up on top like a woman, brought me soup, roast-beef, curry-and-rice, and pepsin melon, this melon growing on trees instead of vines, and digesting the biggest meal almost instantly.

Billed to lecture in the City College, I hired a coolie to haul me there in a rick at so much an hour! To my dismay I found that he was "working" me by the hour, hauling me near the college and turning aside, around and around, for blocks. The hour for the lecture had come and so had the people. In desperation I seized him by the hair and in tones that made his eyes jump, commanded him to take me to the hall immediately or I would execute him on the spot!

WITHOUT A CENT

For a week I was guest of the Good Templars in my own private bungalow in the Cinnamon Gardens, with a servant to bring my meals, and one to look after the house. Around me were millions of strange bugs, butterflies and birds of gaudy hues. Then the ground was of that pleasing red which artists love to mix, much like sienna, that quiets and soothes rather than excites. Cinnamon Gardens must have been the Garden of Eden.

IN THE LAND OF MYSTERY

Entering India at the South, I found bridges and road washed out by recent floods, requiring my going by train to the great Baptist Mission Field at Ongole and Nellore, via Madras, seeing enroute the famous temples at Madura and Trichinopoly where hideously deformed depravity crouched like demons, the very gate of the temple carved with disgusting figures, with sensual orgies inside devoted to the god of Lust.

In a Dak Bungalow built for tourists by the government I lived for a time, and in a double tent. I feared three animals here, the tiger, the scorpion, and the cobra, many thousands of natives dying each year from the bite of the cobra, and other thousands being carried away by the tiger. The sting of the cobra is almost certain death, in great agony, in a few hours. At the home of a missionary where I was entertained a few days, the wife, about to retire, heard a noise in the bed-room, and called for a light. There, near the bed, was a six-foot cobra, standing up from the floor, its ugly flat head swinging from side to side ready to strike. The native servants were called, but they only threw up their hands in horror. Then the husband grabbed a shot-gun and fired, putting out the light, leaving them in total darkness. When a match was hastily struck the cobra was found to have been killed. The natives protect this snake, refusing to kill it, and set a saucer of milk out to it when their own babes are starving, worshipping it as it crawls up

AROUND THE WORLD

to eat. Caught one night in the jungle, I made my way back to town in abject fear lest the next step would bring me within striking distance of the deadly snake that stands on its tail with flattened head as big as your hand, two or three feet above the ground. The scorpion with sting in its tail was also to be feared, as also other animals that bit at both ends. A black scorpion, near my tent, when teased with a cane would roll up his tail over his back and then let it fly just like a whip is cracked, the sting being located, like a bony hook, at the end. Danger from these pests increased when my tent was flooded with water during the monsoon.

But the greatest danger in India is from the sun. "Let A Little Sunshine In," is never sung here. A little of it, through a nail-hole in the roof, striking the head a few minutes, would be disastrous. To cross the street on a cloudy day, bareheaded, might prove fatal. A "sick headache" results from a little sun on the head, temples, or back. You must wear a coat on the hottest days to keep the sun from the backbone! Visitors to the missions seldom heed these warnings, and some of them never get back home.

One morning a native walked in ten miles from the jungle to be married to a girl in the school. His head-dress of sixty yards of cloth with clean shirt and dress were all propped up by a big umbrella close to his skinny wife of eighteen with bracelets, fingerlets, anklets, earlets and noselet, everything but a house-to-let, all of pure iron or brass. The noselet hung just over the mouth and was irremovable, so that when he kisses her he has to "lift up the latch." That evening the newly-weds took their honeymoon on a ten-mile hike. As she grows in character, the heathen rings, on fingers as well as elsewhere, will disappear, there, as in civilized lands; she must teach the folly of the caste system that holds one hundred thousand sets of natives completely under its leaden thrall, writing queer characters in chalk over the

WITHOUT A CENT

forehead or on the doorstep, keeping other castes at a distance of ten feet!

The carpet in heathen homes was of cow-dung plastered over with bare hands, including the steps at the door, and chairs, if any. When this has dried it is the same as if the house had been scrubbed and dusted, when guests may enter. But should you or I enter, or any one not of the caste, the lady of the house must at once on our departure go into the street for a fresh supply of the soft "carpet."

Beautiful for its fine architecture and wide streets, I rode north from Bombay, through a wild jungle, where roads, food and water were hard to find. A native climbed an eighty foot palm to bring down a bunch of cocoanuts from which I ate and drank, their milk being the only safe fluid I could find. Sleeping out and roughing it, with inadequate protection from the sun, I soon felt oncoming illness. A Brahmin invited me to breakfast with him on the floor of his house, with two wide banana leaves several feet long for our dishes on which porridge was served, with milk that I could hardly get into my mouth with my hand for a spoon, he meanwhile extolling the virtues of his Idols, which I was about to accept, on trial, had the milk not chased me about the room, or had not, when I landed some of it in my hand, ran down my arm and over my face. Our dining floor was six inches higher than the other floors because it was the room of the males, while the females occupied a room with floor six inches down!

A MAN-EATING TIGER

The man-eating tiger in India is a frightful foe to natives and tourists. While here, fourteen hundred and six people were devoured by this ferocious beast. Horses in harness had been attacked and killed right in the very suburbs of Bombay. I was miles out in the jungle. Night after night a tiger had robbed a village of its natives. The railroad company, knowing the terror such a beast inspires, offered a big reward to the brave hunter succeeding in killing it. Three Englishmen, armed with Winchesters, accepted the offer, and were carried by the company to the jungle town at the edge of which ran the railroad. Here their special was sidetracked, used as a dwelling by day, and as a fort at night when the tiger usually attacks. The men slept through the day, and with cocked rifles leveled out of the windows that also answered for doors, waited for the man-eater from inside. Two of the hunters, by their commanding position, swept the entire country toward the jungle. The rifle of the other guarded the people as they slept in their shapeless shacks.

The third day came. That afternoon when the men awoke, the idlers around the car said the tiger had gone. No one saw it go, but they were sure it had gone. When night came, however, the men watched as usual. The fourth night, but no tiger. The loafers were surer than ever the tiger had gone, and made fun of the hunters. Half-believing what they said, the men drank more freely of "spirits," to keep off the fever, they said. When night, with its leaden wings outspread, stole over the village, it found the hunters more drunk than sober. But the watch was set.

The stars came out and flooded the jungle with ghostly glimmering of light. The full moon rose shimmering over the coast of Malabar. At ten, quiet and safety reigned over the jungle. At midnight all was well. Liquor had overcome the man on the village side, who was now falling over himself in drunken snooze. The two hunters then decided to doze a little, each taking a nap after the other, the one awake to give the alarm. This game of "Now you sleep and I watch" dragged on until some time between three and four, when all three were in drunken dreams.

And while they slept the tiger came! He sprang

WITHOUT A CENT

through the open window, seized one of the men and was off, the fellow screaming for his life, just as the moon sank behind the cocoanut palms!

All they had to do was to pull the trusty trigger of their forty-eight calibre rifles, and the spotted terror would have spat out his life-blood at the wheels of their coach. That day the news of their killing the man-eater would have flashed all over the country. They would have been worshipped as heroes. Ballrooms, dazzling in Indian splendor, were ready to receive them. The most lovely women of the empire would have been their partners. Receptions at Court, and obeisance in the street, awaited their victorious return.

My curiosity to meet one of these cannibals in his lair was greater than my fear. The crackling of brush ahead startled me, but I believed I could somehow escape. Usually the noise had been made by fleeing deer or chattering monkeys, or by reptiles and smaller prey. The most interesting was the monkey, always in bands, which would take to the smaller trees where they would snarl and make hideous faces. Great flocks of gorgeous parrots flew near. In towering banyan trees fed by hundreds of descending root branches, hung, upside down, mammoth bats, their wings extending feet instead of inches. Now and then a dark native would pop up from the underbrush, surprising me more than all the other wild life, and when I rode into these backwoods villages the natives fled in terror, leaving their huts, unused to a bicycle.

I found some schoolmates as missionaries with whom I spent a night, glad for the sound sleep I hoped to get by their kindness. But during the night the rats raced all over and under my bed, up and down the walls, and even across the ceiling, dropping sometimes to the floor. As I knew them to be carriers of Bubonic Plague then raging, my rest was less satisfactory than it had been in the jungle. At breakfast they wondered how I ever got through the jungle, while I wondered how I got through the night!

At Bulsar I found another schoolmate who "lived by the side of the road and was a friend to man." On Christmas I gave an entertainment arranged by Bishop Stover under a mammoth awning. After a feast that evening, I went on to another town where another schoolmate honored me with a Hindu audience, presided over by the Mayor pulled there in his two-wheeled cart by four lean cows, when the enthusiasm of my big opera-house audience overtaxed my strength. A second Christmas dinner hastened the attack of the fever, but still thinking to throw it off, I ventured into the jungle to study the monkeys.

The big dog that followed me proved to be the sworn enemy of monkeydom. From behind a clump of cactus I watched them at play, holding the dog. The kiddie monkeys were turning somersaults, while a favorite pastime among the young swells was that of picking fleas and lice from each other, which were at once eaten with great relish. Then a growl from the dog scattered them, when mothers picked up their half-grown babies and leaped brush higher than my head, the kid hanging below with its arms about the mother's trunk, its head at her neck, between her arms, its long tail wrapped around her body near the hind legs. Then a big male monkey ran to the top of a tree, calling loudly, as if to say: "Come on!" Soon every monkey of them was in the tree, arranged about him in a circle. Although without Roberts' Rules of Order, it was easy to see that he was the chairman of that assembly. When he finally brought the house to order he told them, not to leave the present field for a more promising place, to scratch his back, or pick a thorn from his foot, but to "get" that dog and stranger. With a whoop the meeting adjourned sine die, as they jumped headlong at us, the cowardly dog, with tail between his legs, setting out for town,

WITHOUT A CENT

leaving me at the mercy of the whole pack of screaming, clawing brutes! I called him to come back, but he ran the faster, while I hit the dust, with monkeys ahead of me, on both sides, and behind, their eyes on the fleeing dog, but making ugly faces at me.

Too weak to run far, I was glad when the pack turned back. The fright and exertion had exacted the last atom of my energy, as I dragged my fainting body back to the mission, when the train hurried me back to St. George's Hospital in Bombay for five weeks of typhoid.

Twice a day I was given a bath by a pretty nurse, which much refreshed me, the bath, I mean. My brain at night was afire with delirium, compelling me to do titanic thinking, big audiences making me discuss with passionate earnestness every question of the day with all the hair-splitting finesse of the philosopher. One day the U. S. Consul came for my name and my father's name and address, so he could ship my body home!

Daylight and doctor, nurse and clean sheets were most welcome. Visitors came, the secretary of the Y. M. C. A., and friend Stover from Bulsar, with fruit. The doctor's visit was best of all. In his natty white suit and sailing cap, he looked health to us patients. He never said quite enough or stayed long enough. Some visitors stayed too long, talked too much, and left a bad suggestion. No patient should be made to argue. They did not realize how very weak I was, and how weak they should appear before me. Paul knew this truth, when he said, "Who is weak and I am not weak?" I liked the visitor who came to my bed in a natural manner as if to do me good and not to steal my pocket-book or upset the bed, who in going left with me a suggestion of joy or encouragement.

While convalescing, one afternoon a tall, handsome English naval officer entered the wide-open veranda and stood looking down upon the empty bed on my right. He first removed his helmet, rattling with decoration and shining with metallic lustre. Then he looked at his coat, blazing with medals of honor, one of them pinned there by the King's own hand. But that had to come off. At last, in hospital pajamas, he drew the light sheet over him. On the other side of the room lay a young Irishman ill with what was supposed at first to be bubonic plague. Next to my left was an English official of Bombay, and down the line wan faces of Germans and Hindus peeped from under white covers. The naval officer looked like the rest of us. For we all look alike under hospital covers and in graveyards!

Books and papers were furnished patients. I read almost constantly, enjoying the Bible and "Livingstone" most. But this officer did not care for books, least of all the Bible.

His disease was peritonitis, so incurable with typhoid in India. He was dying, and his sufferings were very great.

"O dear!" he would cry. "Bring me another drink!"

The nurse was busy, and contrary to the doctor's orders, I arose several times to help him.

At evening two officers came from his battleship to visit their fellow comrades in arms, and asked:

"Have you a message to send to your wife in England, Charles?"

"Yes, officers, in the morning. Come in the morning, won't you?"

"Yes, Charles, we'll be back at five in the morning," they replied.

At nine he was worse. Then the day nurse came. I knew then that someone was going to die, for she never came unless one of the patients was not expected to live till morning.

At ten she came in again and asked if she might send for the chaplain.

WITHOUT A CENT

"No, I don't want the chaplain," he answered.
"May I pray for you?" she asked, timidly.
He seemed to reply in the negative.

A little later she came again and knelt by his side, a prayer-book in her hand, while he moaned and gasped for breath, his temperature at 107. When she began to read the prayer for the dying you could have heard a pin fall at the end of that ward.

At fifteen minutes after one he called for a light.
"Bring me a light! It is getting dark. I want more light!"

Two lights burned near. But the trouble with Charlie was the hand of death passing over his face. The nurse brought another one, holding it right into his face, knowing that its brightness would not hurt his fast dimming eyes.

"Ainsworth! Ainsworth!" he cried, with his last strength. Ainsworth was a rough companion in the third bed down. At the second call he was by his side.

"Hold my hand, Ainsworth, and stand by me!" were his last words.

"I will, Charles!" said he, and he couldn't have let go if he had tried. It was the farewell death grip of two boys far from home!

I limped to his side, hoping I might say a word or pray for him, but he didn't see me. His eyes were focussed at too long a range. They were looking across foaming oceans, burning deserts, snow-capped mountains and great continents!—thinking they saw a little cottage in England, nestling among hawthornes and cherries, in Kent, thinking they were looking through the shutters into that little cottage where the young wife, busy with needle, a little flaxen-haired boy by her side, was now holding a photograph of the long-absent father as he lay dying, ten thousand miles away, in India. That picture was the foreground and we were the background of the sailor officer's last scene on earth.

AROUND THE WORLD

His head fell back. His breathing stopped.

* * * * * * *

At two o'clock he launched his bark upon the Sea of Death! At two o'clock he dared to go before his Captain without a pilot. At two o'clock he ventured into the presence of his Judge without his Christ.

That afternoon at four o'clock the bell tolled thirty times for Charlie as the nurse played on the little organ in the little chapel of our ward, when we heard the TRAMP! TRAMP! TRAMP! of the feet of those who carried Charlie's body out of the ward down to the boat bound for England, going back to the little cottage in Kent!

To add to our terrors, one of our patients, allowed to leave the ward too soon, had overeaten and had returned with a relapse, dying in two days. Another discouragement was the dying right around us daily of eighty to a hundred natives with the plague. We feared to breathe the very air. But I was recovering. On the 18th of February the nurse no longer took my temperature. From a menu of buffalo milk thinned with water I was given egg custard, the supremely best-tasting thing I ever ate. Then beef tea and custard. On the fourteenth day of convalescence I had a small bowl of finely crumbed white bread and milk that tasted a hundred times better than ice-cream to a well man. Next day I had a poached egg and a pint of milk. Seventeen days after the fever I had bread and butter, the crust carefully cut away. Minced boiled fish, boiled potatoes and tapioca followed. Eating an orange one day I could not control my greed for it and swallowed a seed. Instantly I knew what might happen. I could feel that seed like a lump of sharp lead in my stomach and intestines. Fever began to return. I became decidedly uneasy. I told the nurse, who told the doctor. That night the day nurse came just as she had come for Charlie. The doctor came too, more anxious than I. There wasn't much fun or sleep for some of us that night. But I

WITHOUT A CENT

prayed. The next day I knew I was out of danger. I learned to walk again by leaning on two black servants, then with a wheel-chair and with crutches, and then out to face the world again, my hospital bills paid and twenty dollars in my pocket. My daily expense had been only thirty-three cents for everything. St. George's Hospital should be duplicated everywhere. The state, rather than the individual, should look after the sick.

The best mission field was the best workshop. The native must be shown how to make a pair of shoes out of less leather than he puts into a pair for fifty cents, and get five dollars for them. The Hindu sits down to dig a post-hole, and four or five holes is a day's work. A native was running a lathe with his feet; still another with his mouth. A Gujerati woman borrowed the rubber water bottle of my friend to cure the cramps of her grandmother. After the old lady died, which she did, he sent for the bottle. Not coming, he went for it. "Oh!" said the woman, crying, "we had bad luck. We filled it with water and was holding it over the fire when the rubber all fell to pieces!" A doctor pow-wowed for a sick woman. He placed her head on one stump, her feet on another, urging her to maintain her body over the gulf without falling through. Then he set a tub of water on her stomach, the rascal bowing and scraping around her, when she finally broke down, dying soon after. The medical missionary is swamped with patients. Doctoring them is his best opportunity for Christian service. After hearing the mission kiddies sing "Precious Jewels" I went to another part of town and in a heathen school was saddened beyond words when I saw scores of little child-widows not yet twelve years old who never sang, and whose lives were bitter, their hair shorn, jewels taken away, nice clothes replaced by rags, their baby faces marred by hopelessness; mistreated, jeered, beaten by all. To be a missionary in India is the sine que non of ambition.

Passing through a region where marriage takes place in periods of eleven years, when every girl must be married, and if unable to fine a mate a proxy must be substituted until the right man comes along, I rode through the gate of the far-northern city of Delhi and saw the largest Mohammedan mosque in existence, where fifteen marble domes were tipped with gold. At Agra I saw the Taj Mahal three times, morning, noon and night, built as a monument by Shah Jehan over his beautiful wife and queen, Mum-taz-i-Mahal, whom he loved. The delicate beauty of the marble latticework inside is impassably great. The mosque here is lined with pure marble, flowers, fruits and animals of India, being perfectly traced in precious gems, cornelians, rubies, sapphires, agates, diamonds, pearls and emeralds. A dishonest tourist could pick out a handful with his penknife. The floor itself was laid in gems. Preferring the fool's jewels rather than the gems of the mind and the true gold of character, these Mogul kings built well in marble and jewels.

Although it was winter time and in the north, the heat was almost unbearable. The natives travel in great numbers. Every train is filled with them, their heads, arms and oftentimes their legs sticking out of windows. Thousands of them climbed out of the coaches at Benares and other thousands had walked in from the jungle hundreds of miles to bathe in the sacred Ganges. Thousands of these Hindus were bathing in one place near the burning-ghat, the water so slimy with filth, stinking sewers and dead bodies it would make good mucilage. Heathen priests sold this fetid water for so much a ladleful. At this burning-ghat several corpses were partly consumed, then tossed into the river. Other bodies were being carried past the missionary's home, where I stood, with the lady in charge, when she noticed one of the corpses moving his toes. She hurried out to discover that the man was still alive, when she stopped the procession, as the corpse, demurring, sat up. The "dead" man argued with her with such strength as to lead her to assume that he could still be of service in his home. So she demanded that he be taken back.

After a rest in the luxurious Grand at Calcutta, I took the train for the Himalayas, passing through jute and rice fields in the valley, and rising into the cool atmospheres of little mountain towns amid gorgeous foliage and rocks. As if they were the happiest people in the world, the natives smiled at us, even while carrying incredible burdens upon their backs. The little two-foot-track train of cars crosses and recrosses its own track in spirit climbings, my typhoid nerves barely able to enjoy the sudden curves and the seeming indifference the train had of staying on the rails. Great varieties of ferns grew up here on stumps, trunks of trees, and even in the tree-tops, while some trees bore mammoth cluster flowers, of deepest crimson or snowy whiteness.

Darjeeling

With two footmen and a guide I set out on a nervous steed from Hotel Rockville, the only hotel located in a safe position from landslides, to see the highest mountain in the world, Mt. Everest—twenty-nine thousand feet—and then down the mountainside to a tea-estate of fifty thousand acres! The tea is grown on bushes about the size of the raspberry, and trimmed back in such a way so as to dwarf it into many short branches affording the maximum number of small leaves which make the tea. Natives were picking these leaves in baskets for the big hoppers in the "factory" where the "breakers" and "curlers" changed the olive green leaf into shrivelled bits of faded "tea." The smaller the leaves, the better the tea. The very smallest that can be picked make tea that sells for fifty dollars a pound. While there I chose to drink the fifty-dollar variety. On a hill near the Tea Estate I saw some flower-trees at their best, the flowers being as big as your head, white as snow, or red as blood, each complete in sepal, petal, stamen, and pistil, the botanical wonders of the Himalayas.

While descending the mountains we were all but wrecked, as at full speed of nine cars, loaded with tourists on a sharp curve over a precipice, the train was stopped a car-length from a stalled ox-team. If the brakes had not instantly worked, we would have been hurled down from the precipice, thousands of feet. The curve in the track at that place, and the downgrade, together with the nearness of the edge of the mountain wall, made this inevitable. That night we met with another fright, where some Hindus, discharged from the service, spitefully tied steel crowbars across the rails, the sharp flanges of the locomotive wheels cutting the bars in two, and saving us.

EASTER IN BURMA

Forty thousand a week were dying from the plague, ninety-eight per cent fatal, and when I landed at Rangoon, I was ordered to appear before the health officer for ten days—long enough to see the Burmese and their country, the streets aflutter with silks worn by men and women, the natives intelligent and docile, but proud and lazy; where nature's ways had changed, for big melons grew out of trees at the end of branches like an apple, or right from the trunk; and where rubber oozed from the bark of other trees like thin mucilage from a leaking can. Here white ants ate the houses rather than the provisions stored in them. In many houses I saw these ants at work, building their tunnel of clay up the supports, to the joists, and then to the rafters, never showing themselves except when their tunnel of clay is broken, and working usually at night. They feast on the heart of the timber, hollowing and honey-combing it, so that no matter how strong it may look on the outside, and how well painted or polished, it falls with its own weight, when pillar and post, joist and rafter all go down in terrible and complete ruin with the enemy that did it. Fortunately there is one wood, a most excellent kind, too, the teak, which is not bothered by these ants. This wood is used for building purposes, and for furniture.

There is a tree here that has to be licensed, just like a saloon, called the "toddy" palm. It grows in many places in India and may be cultivated in similar warm climates. When an intoxicant is wanted by the owner, or by a passer-by, all he needs to do is to climb into this palm, bore a little hole and hold a vessel to catch the sap, or hang one there while he goes about his work. It is much desired as a drink by those who would otherwise frequent a bar, and a little of it makes a man drunk. I saw hundreds of half cocoanuts and tin cans hanging to these toddy trees to catch the liquor, while natives staggered in circles, near by.

The Baptists were operating a big publishing house in Rangoon, and their missions seem to control the destiny of Burma. Up the Irawaddy, navigable for nine hundred miles, but very treacherous, I found a college-mate as the only missionary in a town of sixty-five thousand, and a parish of three hundred thousand. In his hill bungalow I met two old friends—a Conn Cornet, and a maple-eye dresser, both of which had helped to make my time pass pleasantly in "Old Shurtleff" near St. Louis, and which I sold to him on the eve of his going to Burma.

Cruise Over Equator

On a Chinese liner, the captain invited me to share the "Bridge" with him, where under an awning I was sheltered from the intense sun. The food for the Chinese was cooked in a large iron boiler which was kept going most of the time, as also their chop-sticks in this chop-suey. In the first cabin, awkward Chinese women with remnants of feet pinched into shoes the size of a heel, leaned on two maids with good feet, as they went back and forth from the dining table to a chair. In second cabin, the women, being lower in the scale of Chinese "society" were higher in the useful scale, for with loose sandals, or bare-footed, they walked easily, their beaming faces telling of the inward hope inspired by their freedom.

The Heavens on the Equator were strangely new. In it was the Southern Cross, that I had seen also in India. The Pole Star was only an hour high. In Malacca Strait we passed the Island of Sumatra, and then Borneo, the sun right above our heads, with rays so fierce we dared not look at it. Typhoons gathered and burst about us. Frightfully close, a waterspout formed, magnificent in dimensions and splendid fury. The whirling cyclone of water reached to a height of hundreds of feet, that poured down and sucked up, at the same time, a whirling volume of water, that would have instantly destroyed our ship and all on board. Larger and larger it became, higher and higher it lengthened, until its funnel of solid water was a thousand feet high, with a circumference, at the bottom, of a thousand feet, tapering rapidly to a narrow neck or waist that swayed and bent like a giant rubber hose, enlarging at the top where it joined the clouds, black and ominous, that rolled and fused like contending hosts, the ocean meanwhile churned into violent foam. An old sailor said it was the most terrible one he had ever seen. Two little sail-boats were being drawn into its voracious maw, but as we put on speed, to keep clear of its path, we could not know whether or not they were finally sucked up and lost. At this time there flew on deck a little sparrow pursued by a hawk. It rested for hours in the low-rigging, picking up such food as I offered it, the hawk lurking on the highest mast and getting only what was thrown overboard, which was very hard for it to pick up. The sparrow must have been chased for many hours as it no sooner lighted on the rigging than it fell asleep. One night I was asked by the captain to give a moonlight "reading" on deck. On passing the hat, three silk-clad Mongolians dropped in a silver dollar each.

INDIA AND BURMA

Rocking Baby While Grinding Himalayas

Bringing Down Cocoanuts for Author from 80-Foot Tree

Since Touring World

Hudson R. Road

WITHOUT A CENT

I LAND IN CHINA

Among bleak islands the boat sailed into one of the finest of bays, with Hongkong hanging to the lower side of the island mountains. Here I found the American hotel just far enough up the hill to hide in a cool forest atmosphere. Twenty-course meals and a lot of sleep in a big, airy room, put me in shape for a jaunt into the interior.

On the mainland the roads were easy to ride, but as the guide posts were all in Chinese, I couldn't tell whether I was coming or going. I hired a "coolie" to haul me in his "rick," but neither of us could tell any better where we wanted to go. Our journey came to a halt when, hurrying him along too vigorously, he suddenly dropped the fills, letting me go on—astraddle of his neck. He took the situation rather too seriously to agree with the humor I saw in it, and when I finally extricated myself from his cue and was again seated, I ordered him to "gee" around, and take me back to the beginning of things.

On an all-night steamer ride up the Pearl River to Canton, I was asked to tell of my travels from a box of Quaker Oats. Being the only European aboard, one of their number, who spoke English, acted as my interpreter.

"What is wrong with China?" asked one, as they all waited my answer. I knew what was the matter with that great, ambitious nation, but for some reason I did not say it. I should have said: China, like all promising futures, needs Jesus Christ. Had they evaded my hat when they passed it for a collection as I had evaded that question, I would have been short of change when I landed in Canton. But the poorest among them cast in their mite—a square copper with a hole in it, worth one-sixteenth of a cent.

In the moonlight, and at dawn, I studied the scenery along the river, where hills melted into rolling and then flat land, the higher portions crowned by pagodas. A strange kind of bird sang a song by the river bank, and farmers went about their fields with braided sticks down their backs and funny sacks for coats. I found the same hopes and aspirations in the hearts of these Chinese aboard as you would find among tourists bound for the Dakotas. The little babe hung on the mother's back asleep, while women stroked its forehead or kissed its quivering lips. Venders of peanuts and sugar-cane sticks passed through the crowd. The women were modest and the girls were sweet.

When I walked down the gang-plank I was met by a lank Indiana freshman giving orders there to hundreds of celestials while on his vacation to earn some money, and help China to western ideas. On the other side of the river, Pittsburg locomotives were running around on Carnegie steel-rails, as American foremen were showing Chinamen how to build and run a railroad.

Every street in old Canton was a Barnum side-show. Too narrow for any vehicle except those carried by men, the bewildering maze of swinging signs and jostling natives, compelled me to take a guide. When he took me into a big dry-goods store I thought my last day had come. The doors were instantly closed and locked. The clerks and proprietors all moved toward me, but I stood my ground like a brave man. That's all I could do. If I could have run, I would have done it.

"No chargee for lookee!" they said, as I walked back from the display of rich silks and souvenirs towards the doors, which were politely opened, as I went out and another customer, a lady, came in, the doors closing on her as they had on me, my guide explaining to me this Chinese custom of putting the entire force of salesmen at the service of the customer.

I saw the dirty old temple of five hundred gods; got out of the way of the wheel-barrow hauling a hog on one side and a man on the other; bought candy that was not very good, and some cheap souvenirs; had my meals at the only American hotel; and visited the big penitentiary. As I entered, the big iron gate clanked shut behind me, leaving my guide and myself right in the midst of a most miserable lot of prisoners, most of them chained. I was about to give one of them a coin, when I remembered that I was in China, where the rules and regulations governing criminals were not so humane as our own, and lest I break a law that might commit me also to that very prison, I put the money back into my pocket as with pained face the man drew back a disappointed hand. Out in the Square felons were pilloried by heavy planks on which were printed their names and crimes. Those to be executed in a few days—river pirates—were teased by children, who tickled them on the nose, or kicked them, the victim retaliating with an ugly face, and by spitting at them.

With this out-of-date punishment in my mind I walked out of the big city gate in the old wall, and from the outside saw running over that great wall hundreds of telephone and telegraph wires, bearing the electric impulse of light and love throughout the Empire. Below, in rude niches in the wall, sacred tapers flickered out their fading flame. Half were dead. The others only smoked. Up there, in those wires, the silent servant of Christian faith, in her triumphal chariot of the electric spark, bore the sweet message of Love and Liberty to four hundred millions.

A WEEK IN OUR MANILA

It was good to steam into Manila Bay, where lay our own men-of-war. Behind the city, and on either side, rose bold mountains, dark with foliage, while Cavite, the scene of the Dewey victory, lay eight miles to our right, the old hulk of the Reina Cristina still floating as a souvenir of that breakfast victory. Seeing so many lands not our own, it was inspiring to set my feet on ground looked after by us. I was proud of her lively scenes and new prosperity; to meet our fine officers here, walking so erect and manly, with clear eye and poised self-confidence—the Stars and Stripes flying from the public buildings. At night the Lunette —the park beach—drew a constant stream of pleasure seekers to hear the American band; the Filipino pony, with tantalizingly pretty nostrils and sweet-tempered eyes that flashed the tricky white when desired, and heavy mane that flew about and almost covered the little animal, always present.

In the Y. M. C. A. at Cavite, I read Webster's speech in Congress, when he said he did not believe the settlement of the whites would ever go beyond the Ohio, and when I addressed the soldiers and sailors here we had fun at Webster's expense, for the book, itself, had come all the way across the Ohio, the Mississippi, the Missouri, and all the western states, to San Francisco, where we built a ship, and brought that very book across the Pacific, past Hawaii, to Uncle Sam's victory in the Orient! On the way back to Manila, our launch ran close to the old Spanish wreck, when thrills of inspiration set my blood atingle as I recalled how we changed the tide of western civilization and flung open the door to world-wide dominance in good cheer and glad industry, setting the jewel of Hope agleam upon the brow of our "Little Brown Brother," and turning all eyes toward us as the World-Redeemer!

I Buy a Ticket for Uncle Sam's Country

Our transport Logan lay at the fumigating station loaded with human cargo of soldiers, officers and private citizens homeward-bound, when a movement in the water turned my attention that way. It was an octopus, a yellowish, many-armed fish, partly floating on the surface, whose myriad arms now twirled and wound among themselves as they sought the object interfering with their sea rights. Another sea curiosity was the nautilus—a shell-fish that hoists a tiny sail, and travels hundreds of miles. Soon the sea was full of these little ships, the only ocean-going vessels never sunk by the roughest gale. Catching one, I

WITHOUT A CENT

found it to be a good model of a miniature man-of-war of the Monitor type, with sail set in the middle of the deck at such angle as would maintain its equilibrium, and give it the greatest chance to make headway. Though only a few inches long, it was built for endurance, while its speed astonished the soldiers and others now watching the race between hundreds of them on the high seas.

I bunked low down with the soldiers at twenty-five cents a day, but after nine days I was allowed to change to second cabin, with meals in first cabin, paying fifty cents more a day. There seemed to be too much difference in the quality of the food served the soldiers, and that of the officers and civilians. The boys who fight Uncle Sam's battles deserve the best that their Uncle can give them. Uncle Sam had provided better things for them. It was the red-tape of profiteering whereby one or more individuals in his employ enriched themselves by a "rake-off" at the expense of the boys.

Here is a first-cabin meal: Soup, roast lamb, prime roast beef, roast goose, mashed potatoes, corn, olives, apples, dates, nuts, raisins, plum pudding, strawberry ice cream, cake, coffee, tea.

Our only thrill at sea was when we sighted a big drove of mammoth whales, following each other at regular intervals, a half dozen spouting at the same time, their long, curved backs showing above the water. When the leader saw us he tried to hide with such speed as to make great circles of waves about him that would have easily swamped an ordinary row-boat. Evidently they were on their way to a feeding station, on a course as direct and certain as though guided by compass and transit.

TWO DAYS IN JAPAN

Japan was a new world, unlike anything I had seen, the houses being the most beautiful in lightness and strangeness of architecture. I took four rickshaw rides the first day, and on the second day was pulled out into the country amid flowers and gardens, and fields of real old Japan, where I said "Ohio!" to anyone I met on the road, when I wanted to say "Good morning!" It was queer to be pulled along the country roads by a light-footed steed—my handsome Jap—and then, in a fast trot, over the Japanese bridges built of bamboo. When I came to a steep hill I always walked, more to lighten the burden of my faithful nag than for exercise. He stopped at every tea-house along the road, and I had a cup of tea, with him, in every one of them. The tea was poured by little women who looked like little girls. We were never given cream or sugar for our tea, but as the price of a cup of their best tea was only one sen—a half a cent—I couldn't expect these luxuries. Japanese money was easy to handle, the yen being the unit, and worth about fifty cents.

The Japanese appeared to be more courteous, but not so sincere as the Chinese. Their promise, though more readily made, is not so sure to be fulfilled; their goods, while showing great ingenuity and beauty, were less durable and practicable, veneered and tinselled. In municipal improvements the Japanese excelled the Chinese—such as I saw at Nagasaki—and their sanitary conditions are much better.

ONE DAY IN HAWAII

As soon as the "Logan" anchored in the charming bay I went ashore with my wheel, and rode far out on the excellent roads, amid tropical scenes such as you see in pictures, the summery houses woven with matting like huge flowers gone to seed, sheltered under huge palms, the blue waters of the Pacific gleaming through defiles of bleached volcanic scarf, as natives in "shoestring" shirts waved welcomes, drawing the soft music from ukuleles. As we were about to sail away, soft-eyed girls hung garlands of flowers about the necks of the Americans.

WITHOUT A CENT

Enter the Golden Gate

After three years of travel thrill, my bike and I, that had sailed out of "Hell Gate" on the East, now sailed into "Golden Gate" on the West, San Francisco rising like a fairy wonderland up from the bluest of tranquil bays, where the unexampled enthusiasm of the city's leaders was about to sketch, along a beach unparalleled as a perfect setting, the world's most triumphant exposition.

I landed with TWENTY DOLLARS IN GOLD. No one who has not journeyed far from his native land can imagine just how I felt. Happy is not the word. It is much more than mere happiness. I was in my country. "Breathes there a man with soul so dead, who never to himself has said, 'This is my own, my native land!'"

Featured by the press of the city, and invited to the pulpits of the triune-gemmed bay, San Francisco, Oakland and Berkeley, to tell my travel ramblings in twenty countries, I rode out of the "Hanging Gardens," on June 30, for the fruit farms in California, God's fairest out of doors!

An Unexpected Question

Since "circumpedalling" the globe I have been seriously asked by many young men whether on my travels abroad I did not break the sixth commandment. I have never ridden on a "merry-go-round," been shaven by a barber, smoked my second cigarette, or taken the name of God in vain.

I want to be physically and morally able to win the girl God has for me. My chances for doing this will be best if I live a true life. I have felt the indescribable thrill of "falling in love," and I know there is no other joy or force so overwhelming, so commanding, so uplifting and so superior to the mere physical attraction upon which it may be based. Innocence in love is the most inexpressibly wonderful of all earthly joys. Since the course of true love does not seem to run smooth, I have been tempted, with all others, when the higher seemed unattainable, to accept the lower. But I have refused the one, if I may not have the other, the higher. The girl and boy who steal these sweets, lose infinitely more than they gain, for lust robs of that fine flower of modesty, substitutes a tricky countenance of suspicion for one of frank openness, takes much of the sweetness and power from the voice, and weakens the imagination, reasoning and judgment. It closes the door of ambition and warps every sinew of life. It deprives of the supreme quality of leadership, intellectual and moral initiative, and brings the victim down to the beast, where desire for higher things becomes too weak to gain them. The most disgusting of all sinners is the libertine or adulterer.

Miracles of achievement are possible only to the pure. They can do the impossible. The love of a good girl, in the life of the right kind of man, seals him from temptation by lower desires. If he isn't the right kind of man, and his love for her does not transform him, with her as his only object of feminine affection, he is unworthy of her.

I have refrained, young gentlemen, for at least six reasons: For the sake of a probable future wife and children; to avoid trouble growing from such sin; to become skilled in the highest accomplishments; to preserve strength of character; to avoid disease; to honor God.

I will enumerate here my modest achievements thus far: Graduated high school course with honor, four years; worked my way through and graduated college course with honors, four years; worked my way through last year (1911) university course, divinity and literary, three years; worked my way around the world alone, three years; Chautauqua and lyceum platform, two years; movie theatres, six months; worked my way from Chicago to San Francisco in

WITHOUT A CENT

one hundred towns, one year; worked my way South, three months.

During all of this time and up to this date, December 15, 1921, I have not technically broken the sixth commandment. My strength and endurance is increasing rather than lessening. I can swim ten times farther now than during my college days, and can run twenty times farther with less effort.

* * * * * * *

From Leland Stanford University, the flower of a night's heartbreak, I wheeled into Santa Clara Valley and hired out to pick apricots and prunes, eating myself full and picking some besides.

I saw the Golden State from one end to the other on its beautiful roads, the best on earth, and hiked over its mountains to look down upon a myriad of fairy cities whose prosperous splendor would have made the Promised Land look like a deserted desert, bathed in its tropical ocean surf, lived with the people in their idyllic homes and was entertained at her munificent hotels.

On the sublime Sierras I sailed on Lake Tahoe's magic waters, where mountain scene and tint of lake vie with wonders abroad, a lake twenty-one miles by eight, fifteen hundred feet deep. I saw the "bucking bronchos" and cow-girls ride on bare-backed bulls; the limitless land left waiting the energetic easterner, the ten-thousand-acre farms that ought to be cut up into many homes; the Colorado Rockies and her dashing rivers, to the great Father of Waters, to Illinois, where after three years facing the East I was greeted at the west door of our home by my mother!

My 40,000-mile thrill had ended! I had cycled the globe!

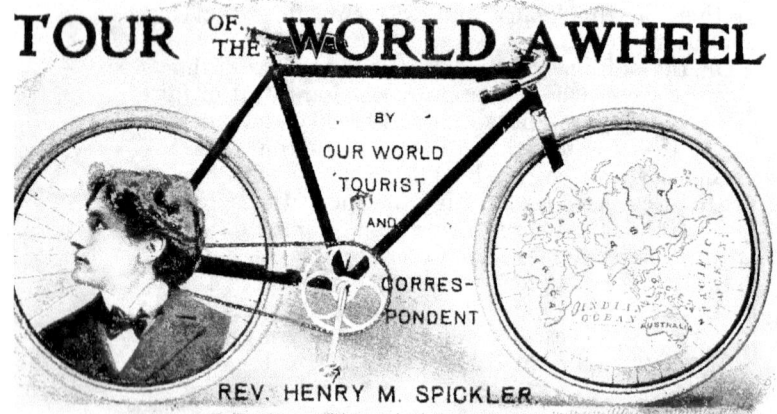

www.ingramcontent.com/pod-product-compliance
Lightning Source LLC
LaVergne TN
LVHW051553070426
835507LV00021B/2561